T0383949

Prophetic Peril

RACE
RHETORIC
& MEDIA

Davis W. Houck, Series Editor

Prophetic Peril

The Rhetoric of Nineteenth-Century African American Prophetic-Call Narratives

Thomas M. Fuerst

UNIVERSITY PRESS OF MISSISSIPPI / JACKSON

The University Press of Mississippi is the scholarly publishing agency of
the Mississippi Institutions of Higher Learning: Alcorn State University,
Delta State University, Jackson State University, Mississippi State University,
Mississippi University for Women, Mississippi Valley State University,
University of Mississippi, and University of Southern Mississippi.

www.upress.state.ms.us

The University Press of Mississippi is a member
of the Association of University Presses.

Copyright © 2025 by University Press of Mississippi
All rights reserved
Manufactured in the United States of America
∞

Library of Congress Cataloging-in-Publication Data

Names: Fuerst, Thomas M., author.
Title: Prophetic peril : the rhetoric of nineteenth-century African
American prophetic-call narratives / Thomas M. Fuerst.
Other titles: Words from elsewhere
Description: Jackson : University Press of Mississippi, [2025] |
Series: Race, rhetoric, and media | Revised version of the author's thesis (doctoral)—
University of Memphis, 2022, under the title: Words from elsewhere:
the rhetoric of nineteenth-century African American prophetic call narratives. |
Includes bibliographical references and index.
Identifiers: LCCN 2024048180 (print) | LCCN 2024048181 (ebook) |
ISBN 9781496855442 (hardback) | ISBN 9781496855435 (trade paperback) |
ISBN 9781496855459 (epub) | ISBN 9781496855466 (epub) |
ISBN 9781496855473 (pdf) | ISBN 9781496855480 (pdf)
Subjects: LCSH: Stewart, Maria W., 1803–1879. | Allen, Richard, 1760–1831.
| Foote, Julia A. J., 1823–1900. | Turner, Nat, 1800?-1831.
Classification: LCC BX6455.S76 F84 2025 (print) | LCC BX6455.S76 (ebook)
| DDC 277.308/1092396073—dc23/eng/20241207
LC record available at https://lccn.loc.gov/2024048180
LC ebook record available at https://lccn.loc.gov/2024048181

British Library Cataloging-in-Publication Data available

For Cassie
I love you like nerds love citations.

Contents

Preface: Words That Create Worlds

In Genesis 1, the God who creates the cosmos *speaks* it into existence. "Speaking, or *davar*, is the touchstone notion in the Hebrew Bible."[1] The anonymous poet writes that God speaks, names, or blesses fifteen times.[2] Thus, for the Jewish and Christian traditions, creation's existence and meaning rise out of a creative rhetorical act, which invites human imitation.[3] Like God's speech, human speech can create meaning from chaos, divide this from that, shed light or shroud in darkness, assign function or nonfunction, cultivate life or death, name or anonymize, and bestow or withhold dignity. Like the Creator, the human creator relates to and manages creation through rhetoric. Kenneth Burke calls humanity the "symbol-using animal"[5]—but more than that, humanity *is* the symbol, the image, the rhetorical act of the Divine Rhetorician. The former expresses a function; the latter, a being.[6]

More than a mere poem, Genesis 1 performs rhetorical and ideological criticism at the opening of the Bible. It offers an alternative ideology—one of monotheism and its accompanying moral implications—to the dominant ideologies of the Babylonian Empire—with its polytheism and moral pluralities.[7] "It serves as a refutation of the Babylonian theological claims,"[8] both oppressing and enticing the exilic Jewish communities. Whereas Babylonian creation poems describe the formation of the world via theomachy—a war of the gods—Genesis 1 describes creation through a peaceful, nonviolent, noncoercive *rhetorical* moment.[9] No one among many or god of the philosophers, Israel's deity is something like "*nommo*, the life-giving mystical force offered through verbal and vocal discourse."[10] This discursive deity speaks, and creation opens itself, as an audience, to listen and respond. Rhetoric drives the relationship between Creator and creation such that creation remains free to accept or reject the invitation.[11] In contrast to the coercive and chaotic creation myths of Babylon, Genesis 1 describes a deity who does not demand response.[12] "The universe was not caused, but created."[13] Reply is merely invited but joyfully received.[14]

Thus, the rhetorical resistance of Babylonian mythology resonates as political, persuasive, pragmatic, and, indeed, prophetic. It modifies the material conditions of the cosmos; it "shapes creation in an action which alters reality."[15] Rhetoric moves the material world and removes "the veil of anonymity from the workings of history."[16] The poem does not merely rhetorically demythologize Babylonian religion but therein demystifies Babylonian social, political, and even rhetorical hierarchies. The rhetorical and military violence that justified Babylonian imperial power loses its divine sanctioning. The imperial hierarchy and its hegemonic state rhetoric lose their divine authorization. The rhetorically constructed ideologies of empire lose their divine endorsement. The material effects of Babylonian mythology on everyday life lose their divine approval as the words wielded by the Creator create harmony that displaces disharmony and order that overcomes disorder.[17]

Moreover, Genesis 1 not only rhetorically deconstructs the Babylonian imperial order but also rhetorically reconstructs an alternative community—a counterpublic energized by the God who speaks even in chaos, colonialism, and exile.[18] The poem certainly offers a "critique of domination" by questioning the myths and rhetoric that contribute to the interest of the ruling class and empower their dominance.[19] Further, the poem removes the shield of the "taken for granted" so that it can "expose the discourse of power in order to thwart its effects in a social relation."[20] But these actions of negation also have a constitutive effect. A community of resistance is forged through an affirming identity of divine *chosenness*. The poet has torn away the curtain of Babylonian hegemony and revealed mere *humans* standing on the other side, creating space for a counternarrative of humanity and creation.

Genesis 1 performs something like an ancient socioreligious form of rhetorical criticism via aesthetics, alliteration, cadence, metaphor, intertextuality, and narration. Though, the ancient Hebrews may have just called it prophetic critique: the positing of a counterstory that implies inevitable theological and "moral inducements,"[21] which then shape a community of resistance—communities like the nineteenth-century Black church.

Voices of resistance—prophetic voices—in African American communities have often risen from within religious communities, particularly the church. These voices, like the Divine Rhetorician of Genesis 1, create meaning out of the chaos of the African American experience; argue for the inclusion of Blackness in the *this* when whiteness have forced them to be a *that*; proclaim the divinity of the dark skin vis-à-vis the blue-eyed Jesus of whiteness; assign function and agency in a world denying their right to breathe; name themselves, rename themselves, assert their names, and even subvert the names forced upon them by their oppressors; and, indeed, demand dignity for Black communities, claiming that the divine image spoken in Genesis 1 speaks the language of prophecy.

Prophetic Peril

A Perilous Introduction

Clearly, the Holy Spirit had abandoned the Rev. Richard Williams. In 1818, he stood before the historic Black congregation at Mother Bethel African Methodist Episcopal (AME) Church in Philadelphia as that week's guest preacher. Per the formalities, he began by praying, entreating the Lord to help him expound Jonah 2—a poem penned by Jonah from within the sea monster's belly. Yet as Reverend Williams endeavored to preach, one audience member observed that "he seemed to have lost the spirit."[1] The Spirit, which had pursued obstinate Jonah to the ocean floor, did not deign to step onto the stage that morning at Mother Bethel. Who would save Williams from his homiletical humiliation?

Jarena Lee knew well of Holy Spirit empowerment. She had experienced something of a spiritual high mere days before when she attended to a young man on his deathbed. Prior to his illness, he resisted the good news of Lee's gospel. With mortality at his doorstep, however, he asked for her by name. After arriving, she prayed for him, and with her eyes still closed, she saw Jesus in cruciform posture resting just above his head. As he began to lose consciousness, he accepted the pardon for sins Lee had proclaimed through Jesus Christ. Indeed, as his spirit departed, all present celebrated his conversion and the knowledge that his soul had secured rest.

Successful in her Spirit-led evangelism, Lee now recoiled at the Spiritless preacher standing before her. Eight years before, in 1810, the Rev. Richard Allen had denied her the denominational rights to preach. The AME *Book of Discipline* had no need for, nor did it permit, women preachers. At the time, Allen's rebuff affirmed Lee's own skepticism that no one would believe Jesus had called her. It also alleviated some of her fear about the daunting nature of the task. She had, after all, not only argued with Jesus over the calling but, at one point, even concluded Satan, rather than God, had spoken to her. In the end, it took audible voices, vivid dreams, and several timorous trips to Allen's front door before she finally drew up the nerve to knock and tell him of her call to preach. His quick denial corroborated her doubts.

While Allen's refusal initially relieved Lee's "cross," she soon realized her acceptance of his words and abandonment of Jesus's calling sat ill in her soul. She sensed the snuffing out of a holy fire for the conversion of souls, which terrified her more than either denominational doctrines or pastoral denial. After all, had not Mary preached the gospel after witnessing the empty tomb? Does not the entirety of the Christian faith rest on the proclamation of a woman who saw her savior resurrected? Indeed, Christ is no half savior; he died for both men and women.

So why should only men preach? And why should men who have clearly lost the Spirit preach at all? If Reverend Williams cannot expound a text under the empowering of the Spirit, then someone else should do so for the sake of God's people. To help him would alleviate his humiliation, fulfill her calling, and incarnate Jonah 2's claim that "salvation is of the Lord."

A supernatural impulse sprang up within Lee's soul, compelling her to rise up and onto the stage. Taking cues from the Holy Spirit and Jonah 2, Lee preached with such fervor, conviction, and skill that no one could deny her calling. Even Reverend Allen changed his mind and confirmed her prophetic mantle. Like Jonah, she had fled from it, denied it, and doubted it. Like Jonah, her surrender to it resulted in the repentance of the masses. Unlike Jonah, who descended into the realm of death in his resistance, Lee, a woman, merely needed to ascend the stage and finish a man's job for him.

Prophetic Peril explores the rhetorical strategies and storytelling used in the African American prophetic tradition of the nineteenth century, specifically the strategies employed in the prophetic-call narratives of Maria W. Stewart, Nat Turner, Julia Foote, and Richard Allen. Like Jarena Lee, these figures anchor their prophetic messages in the claim that the creator God has called them to the prophetic task of reimagining what *is* and casting a vision for what *could be*. Their calling assumes the God who spoke in Genesis 1 still speaks today and that this speaking materially matters to local communities under the thumb of oppression. Indeed, the language of calling assumes God's speaking has material (not just spiritual) effects in the world. In short, God has called them to criticize systems of oppression and energize countercommunities of resistance, just as the ancient Jewish and Christian prophets did.[2]

PROPHECY AND CALL NARRATIVES

Prophecy's heritage arises from ancient Jewish and Christian rhetorical categories rather than Greco-Roman or Western individualist ones. Owing to this, we must avoid assessing it primarily via traditions foreign to its intentions and norms. By allowing prophecy to speak on its own terms, we gain insights into its distinct contributions to our understanding of speechmaking and persuasion.

For example, contrary to foundational elements of Western speech analysis, the prophetic messenger in the biblical tradition contributes none of the speech's inventive material. Instead, prophetic speech is "incomprehensible except as the speech of a divine messenger; the prophet, properly understood, speaks for another."[3] Prophets essentially "read from a script" handed to them rather than devised by them.[4] Western categories that reduce the speaker to individual charisma or oratorical skills cannot make sense of a genre where the individual becomes a mouthpiece of a divine agent rather than the inventor of the speech.

The complications further increase because the divine agent speaks publicly and politically but not civilly. The script handed to the prophet calls for and creates a community of defiance against the dominant political powers. Yet prophecy joins the political discourse by contributing not reason and rationality but poetry and narratives—like call narratives—that challenge commonsense reasoning. Because the powers are so evil, evil so oppressive, and oppressors so intransigent, "it makes no sense to talk of 'practical wisdom,' 'sensitivity to the occasion,' 'opportunistic economizing,' 'the capacity to learn from experience,' 'flexibility and looseness of interest,' or 'bargaining.'"[5] A prophetic calling has been received; to change the message for political opportunism or to make it more palatable to the audience violates the character of the calling. Western Enlightenment emphasis on prudent, pragmatic attentiveness to civil cohesion has no place in prophetic rhetoric's decided rejection of what the audience deems prudent. Prophetic messengers adamantly refuse to adhere to audience expectations and insist on upturning, rather than affirming, the audience's value system. The audience's value system—its most foundational assumptions about how the world works—after all, is precisely what God called on the prophet to criticize.[6]

For example, scholars have long noted the antipatriarchal potential latent within prophetic rhetoric. The Hebrew Bible, New Testament, and Christian tradition all endorse female prophetic figures. Kerith M. Woodyard even calls for a de-patriarchalizing of prophetic studies, proposing instead a "prophetic liberating principle."[7] Woodyard explores Elizabeth Cady Stanton's *The Woman's Bible* as an example of nineteenth-century feminist prophecy, showing how Stanton suffered rejection from both patriarchists and suffragists, who deemed her prophetic posturing and unapologetic feminist interpretations of biblical texts too radical. Stanton's failure to persuade—indeed, her provoking of her audience to aggression—means her prophetic message failed by any Western notion of successful speechmaking rooted in patriarchy and persuasion.[8] However, because prophecy operates with ancient Jewish prophetic ethos, pathos, and Logos, it does precisely what Stanton intended: it tells the truth about women's experiences of injustice no matter the personal risk or possibility of persuasion. She thus "calls for a fundamental *reordering* of the audience's value system as a means to alleviate social injustice and replicate the natural ordering of creation."[9] Woodyard thus makes the compelling case that by neglecting women's prophecy, we amplify our patriarchal assumptions around the Bible and its interpreters, thereby neglecting "some of the most radical voices in American public address, such as those belonging to female radicals and radicals of color."[10]

James Darsey's otherwise fantastic book *The Prophetic Tradition and Radical Rhetoric in America* reveals the racial oversight Woodyard points out. When discussing the collapse of prophetic impulse in American politics, Darsey comments:

> What the contemporary right has in common with the prophetic tradition is the impulse to order. . . . But there is a considerable difference between an order that derives from compassion, is optimistic, and provides direction for the future and one that derives from fear, is faithless, and retreats into the mythical past. . . . Modern movements of the left are no less spiritually impoverished than that of the right. . . . [Leftist] visions failed to capture the imagination of most Americans not because of any inherent defect, but because radicalism is cultural and these ideals were not of our culture.[11]

Here, Darsey misses the existence of a radical prophetic tradition that asserts the order of justice and appeals to traditions and myths rooted in the American experience. The Black church's prophetic tradition and call narratives offer the possibility of a radical rhetoric transcending right-left dichotomies precisely by refusing to retreat into a mythical past. Rather, Black prophecy demands material political changes within the polis by telling witnessing to—telling the truth about—morally significant events.

Andre E. Johnson argues that this truth telling challenges both white conservatives and liberals, who have historically responded in racial solidarity and intransigence when criticized by Black voices. Prophets know of this obstinacy from the moment they receive their calling, which explains not only their own resistance to the call but also why we must evaluate the "success" of Black prophecy by some other means than persuasion.[12] For prophets in the traditions springing from the biblical text, fidelity in truth telling matters far more than mere persuasion.

This prophetic emphasis on truth telling about, or witnessing, morally significant events arrives in the modern world through, not surprisingly, Jewish Holocaust literature. Elie Wiesel wrestles with his reason for writing *Night* in its preface: "Why did I write it? Did I write it so as *not* to go mad or, on the contrary, to *go* mad in order to understand the nature of madness, the immense, terrifying madness that had erupted in history and in the conscience of mankind?"[13] He settles, instead, on the act of witnessing. He refers to himself as a "witness who believes he has a moral obligation to try to prevent the enemy from enjoying one last victory by allowing his crimes to be erased from human memory."[14] Wiesel implicitly notes that persuasion and witness have different *teloi*: "deep down, the witness knew then, as he does now, that his testimony would not be received. After all, it deals with an event that sprang from the darkest zone of man."[15] Those who witness would prefer their words persuade their hearers, but they know the futility of expecting it.

TYPES OF BLACK PROPHECY

Appreciating the shift from *persuasion* to *witness* matters when attempting to explore *types* of Black prophecy. For example, the two subsets of prophecy given the most attention are *apocalypse* and *jeremiad*. In particular, the jeremiad relies on an agreed upon *covenant* between the prophet and the audience. As the biblical prophet Jeremiah called Israel back to its covenantal obligations with Yahweh, so all jeremiads use some covenant as a moral basis from which the prophet feels the audience has strayed and must return. In Hebrew prophecy, the covenant came directly from God to Moses, and prophets draw on its obligations and invitations for their later critiques and visions. Andre E. Johnson notes, however, that in the case of the African American prophetic tradition, the Constitution of the United States functions as the covenant basis for Black prophecy. In this instance, the covenant both contains the liberative promises and oppressive problems for Black liberation. Thus, many Black prophetic figures expect the covenant to reinforce audience intransigence, which therefore requires them to "develop other forms of prophetic discourse to appeal to and move their audiences."[16]

Relying on the jeremiad as a basis, Johnson defines *prophetic rhetoric* as "discourse grounded in the sacred and rooted in a community experience that offers a critique of existing communities and traditions by charging and challenging society to live up to the ideals espoused while offering celebration and hope for a brighter future."[17] Prophecy may create identity, provide self-worth, inspire to action, or simply "speak out on behalf of others and chronicle their pain and suffering."[18] Regardless, its agenda does not always assume the possibility of persuasion.

Christopher Z. Hobson contributes to our definition of *prophecy* by demonstrating how the complexity and pluralities of the African American prophetic tradition draw from what Gerhard von Rad calls "saving history"[19]—this-worldly action of God to liberate the oppressed. Hobson argues that this closely resembles "African American ideas of God's action in history on behalf of the powerless" and has important parallels in the kinds of rhetoric used by Black prophetic figures.[20] In the Exodus-Deuteronomy tradition, for example, Black prophetic figures use Exodus-related imagery to highlight God's work of liberation in the context of American slavery and racism. The emphasis in this tradition lies in the eventual change in the African American experience. The covenantal ideas in the Exodus-Deuteronomy traditions in the Bible get translated in the African American prophetic tradition as a scathing indictment of America for breaking the sacred covenant by violating the civil rights of Black communities and individuals.[21]

In the Isaiah-Ezekiel tradition, Black prophecy emphasizes its communal hope for eventual restoration.[22] Black restoration comes about through the biblical idea of *turning* or *repentance*. White America has the primary burden of turning,[23] and Black America becomes its own means of redemption when working for its own liberation and speaking the truth of turning to white America.

The Jeremian tradition, Hobson notes, draws on the prophet Jeremiah's conception of a community so hardened by sin that it cannot turn.[24] The African American prophetic tradition herein understands the United States as obstinate, and while expressing hope for white America's turning, it denies its likelihood. Eventually, the hardness of white America's heart results in the nation's downfall.

Finally, Hobson describes the Daniel-Revelation tradition as an apocalyptic prophetic strain emphasizing the approaching end of earthly kingdoms and the inauguration of a new kingdom of God's rule.[25] Through the transition from the present age to the kingdom of God, this tradition challenges Black Americans to endure and persevere. Accordingly, some tensions may exist within the community regarding whether they can expect justice in this life or the next. Turning is not the primary goal of apocalypse, but as long as one hears the prophecy, turning still remains a possibility.

PROPHETIC IMPIETY:
THE IMPLICATIONS OF PERILOUS PROPHECY

Despite Senator Barack Obama's decision to downplay his pastor's rhetoric, despite his analogy that Rev. Jeremiah Wright is the outspoken uncle we all have in our families, and despite his claim that his home church largely avoids controversy, the American media could not ignore Reverend Wright's inflammatory 2003 sermon "Confusing God and Government," where Reverend Wright declares, "God damn America."[26] The pairing of *God* and *damn* already carries a natural feeling of irreverence and impiety, but then when he adds *America* as the target of his damning denunciation, Wright takes a prophetic posture against nationalism. It mattered little to Wright's (or Obama's) critics that his statement was followed by concrete examples of America's exploitative and murderous economic and racist policies. The mere combination of those three words—from a preacher no less—was an intolerable impiety.

Wright's rhetoric was, indeed, impious, but in a deeper way than his critics understood. During a speech, an audience's expectations regarding "what properly goes with what" derive from what Burke calls *piety*.[27] Piety compels the speaker to choose what she deems the appropriate genre or form of discourse in a particular speaking situation. By opting for appropriate means, the speaker identifies with their audience and thus potentially persuades them. However, as noted, the problem with prophecy lies in its refusal to attend to the constrictions of audience expectations, its disinterest in audience notions of appropriateness. Prophecy often opts for an *impious* posture toward the audience, toward what the audience holds sacred, or even toward what most effectively persuades.[28] Goddamn persuasion. Goddamn the audience insofar as they represent and support the systems of oppression.

Reverend Wright's choice of an off-limits curse combining the sacred (God), the sacrilegious (damn), and the secular (America) was no mere expression of tactless rhetorical rage. Wright chose more than impious words; he placed those impious words in a pious form of speech: a sermon. Prophets do such rhetorical maneuvering regularly. They pack pious forms with impious language or impious forms with pious language.[29] The interplay of piety and impiety generates endless possibilities for creativity, allowing prophets to look outside even the piously pious structures of religious language into the so-called secular sphere to transcend the constraints of the sacred, particularly when the dominant discourse has coopted the sacred. The form the prophet chooses does not merely reveal a message. It responds to "perceived situational demands"[30] by stuffing the impious message with unexpected potentialities, alternative social possibilities, and limitations on the available applications.[31]

However, the prophet does not employ forms foreign to the audience. They choose unforeseen forms. As seen in Wright's "Goddamn America" sermon, prophets aim to shock, agitate, and throw off the audience's equilibrium by utilizing forms of lament when expected to rejoice, celebration when expected to mourn, delight when expected to despair, anguish when expected to hope, or damnation when expected to bless. In short, prophetic figures use a variety of tactics[32] to break conventional pieties and invoke "consciousness raising"[33] in the oppressed. The prophet chooses the unforeseen form to raise questions in a world of false answers, cast doubt on unwarranted certitude, or even provide a different orientation toward reality than that arranged by the hegemonic, imperial disorientation of the dominant consciousness's pieties.

Oddly enough, because the prophet does not create the message but rather receives it, they may not even foresee the impiety:

> Neither previous faith nor any other personal endowment had the slightest part to play in preparing a man who was called to stand before Yahweh for his vocation. He might by nature be a lover of peace, yet it might be laid upon him to threaten and reprove, even if, as with Jeremiah, it broke his heart to do so. Or, if nature made him prone to severity, he might be forced, like Ezekiel, to walk the way of comforting men and saving them.[34]

Thus, whether poetry or prose, disputation or dialogue, the prophet's choice contradicts the expectation of form to set before the audience alternatives they had not already considered or they had insisted on *not* considering. Impiety is prophecy's piety; inappropriateness is the prophet's appropriateness. All of this has profound implications for our understanding of prophesy, call narratives, and their discursive functions.

IMPLICATION NUMBER ONE:
GAINING AUTHORITY THROUGH INCARNATIONAL ENACTMENT

In both their call narratives and their subsequent prophetic utterances, prophets rhetorically combine form and content through embodiment or enactment of their impiety. That is, the prophet "incarnates the argument, *is* the proof of the truth of what is said."[35] As von Rad notes, "not only the prophet's lips but also his whole being were absorbed in the service of prophecy."[36]

The force of such enactment is seen in its visual components. The biblical prophet Ezekiel bound himself in ropes to symbolize the eventual bondage of Israel. He also built a model of the city of Jerusalem and theatrically preenacted its besiegement. Most impiously to ancient (and modern) sensibilities, he cooked his meals over a fire of human excrement to symbolize the unthinkable and impious idea that God refuses to protect Jerusalem from foreign invasion.

I explore a similar enactment in chapter 1 as I attend to the rhetorical structure of Maria W. Stewart's call narrative. In the way she structures her narrative, she positions herself rhetorically, spiritually, and physically in the prophetic traditions of Moses, Isaiah, and Paul. In chapter 2, we see how Richard Allen literally "labors" for the gospel in a way that enacts his spiritual authority and criticizes the lack of labor among white clergymen. Chapter 3 highlights Julia Foote's sensual visionary experience wherein she (re)enacts the scene where Jesus washes his disciples feet to show what true power looks like. However, she impiously takes the position of Jesus, thus offering proof of her own messiah-like status. Finally, in chapter 4, Nat Turner's impending martyrdom combined with his childhood call and communal affirmation utilize enactment of biblical messianic imagery to verify his prophetic status.

In both the biblical tradition and the African American prophetic tradition, the *bodily, visual* form of prophetic rhetoric enacts or incarnates the message conveyed. Through enactment, prophets maintain cohesion between message and messenger, between form and content, which enables them to bypass rational constraints and become *proof* of the validity of their message.[37] The frequency of the use of enactment, then, points to the need for analyzing prophecy as a genre.

IMPLICATION NUMBER TWO:
A PERILOUS WAY, A PERILOUS TIME

Jeremiah stood before a stunned crowd in Jerusalem. Their previous preachers had promised peace, assured them they had nothing to fear. But before them stood a prophet advising them to flee their city, imploring them to build siege ramps, warning them of the overflowing wrath of God. Jeremiah accused their preachers of deceiving them about the impending doom, promising "peace, peace, when there is no peace," when in truth, God had damned Jerusalem. The audience expected sermons of affirmation and tranquility; Jeremiah impiously offered denunciation and destruction. Prophecy's penchant for impiety makes it an inherently subversive genre, a subversion that cannot be understood merely by seeing genre as the study of the form words take in a speech. Genre is a social action.

Carolyn R. Miller's 1984 article "Genre as Social Action" argues that genres do not exist in the abstract, awaiting application in concrete situations. Rather, speakers create genres when they apply particular forms in *recurring* situations.[38] These forms, over time, become restraints upon speakers by establishing audience expectations about what is *pious* in a given context. Thus, genres have a social impact. They demand that if the rhetor wants to identify with and persuade an audience, they must take the genre's constraints and audience expectations seriously. Charismatic members of the community may employ creative means to subvert the audience's expectations and the genre's constraints, but they still must know the constraints and expectations before doing so.

The recurrence of types, the audience's expectations, and the constraints upon the speaker bring us to the first difficulty prophecy poses for assessing it as a genre. Despite postmodernity's complication of Western notions of time, we still operate with a linear view. However, as von Rad notes, ancient "Israel's perception of time was taken from a different angle from ours. . . . Hebrew completely lacks a word for our modern concept of time."[39] Israel's conception of time revolved around their festal seasons, which gave rhythm to ancient life, and "the festivals, not time, were the absolute data, and were data whose holiness was absolute."[40] While not sharing a cyclical view of time with their ancient Near Eastern neighbors, Israel's festal-centric conceptions of chronology bound Israel to *historical events*, not mythical ones. As von Rad notes, "When Israel ate the Passover, clad as for a journey, staff in hand, sandals on her feet, and in the haste of departure, she was manifestly doing more than merely remembering the Exodus: she was entering into the saving event of the Exodus itself and participating in it in a quite 'actual' way."[41] Miller's conception of genre assumes a linear notion of time where events in the past are only folded over into the present via analogy, but Israel's notion of time allows for present persons to participate in—indeed, reenact—historical events. Even if understood analogically, Israel's chronology still revolves primarily around its festivals commemorating historical saving events, in which the contemporary community participates. The ritual and liturgies accompanying these festivals created audience expectations and thus pieties connecting the past to the future and present and the present and future to the past.

Thus, given the centrality of Israel's festivals and the prophetic penchant for impiety-as-piety, inappropriateness as appropriateness, we expect and indeed see prophets criticizing Israel's festivals:

When you come to appear before me, who has asked this of you, this
trampling of my courts? Stop bringing meaningless offerings! Your
incense is detestable to me. New Moons, Sabbaths and convocations—
I cannot bear your worthless assemblies. Your New Moon feasts and
your appointed festivals I hate with all my being. They have become
a burden to me; I am weary of bearing them. When you spread out
your hands in prayer, I hide my eyes from you; even when you offer
many prayers, I am not listening. Your hands are full of blood![42]

Since Israel's festivals and sacrifices reincarnate the original saving event
and since that time folds over on itself so that worshipers participate in the
historical event they ritually reenact, prophetic criticism impiously interrupts
Israel's notions of time and communal belonging through time. However,
when prophets criticize Israel's festivals, they do not see themselves as fall-
ing outside the saving history these festivals represent. Rather, they see the
message as bringing new meaning to old categories. Speaking within specific
historical circumstances (kairos), prophets reinterpret the historical saving
events with a new possibility that transcends and supersedes ancient meanings. Herein lies the value of Miller's emphasis on analogous types:

The prophetic message differs from all previous Israelite theology,
which was based on the past saving history, in that the prophets
looked for the decisive factor in Israel's whole existence—her life
and her death—in some future event. Even so, the specific form of
the new thing which they herald is not chosen at random; the new
is to be effective in a way which is more or less analogous to God's
former saving work.[43]

The former festival and ritual become analogous to a new era created via
divine speech, much like divine speech creates a world previously marked
by chaos in Genesis 1.

Keeping in mind that prophetic speech, from the prophet's perspective,
originates in "a divine understanding of human situations,"[44] interpreters
assess four circumstances in which prophetic rhetoric appears in the Hebrew
Bible: (1) syncretism and the dissolution of Yahwism; (2) the institution of
monarchy and centralized power in Israel through the demotion of theocracy;
(3) socioeconomic oppression in Israel; and (4) the rise of oppressive imperial powers outside of Israel.[45] In the African American prophetic tradition,
I add two related elements: (5) the justice of God in history; and (6) God's
identification with the oppressed against the oppressor.[46]

These situations have in common a hierarchical abuse of power. Thus, as
a genre, prophetic rhetoric appears as a response to the recurring presence of
hegemonic, hierarchical discourse and deed, characterized by "control over
the rhetorical territory through definition, establishment of a self-perpetu-
ating initiation or *rite de passage*, and the stifling of opposing discourse."[47]
At every level, prophecy imperils imperial intentions. It questions or rejects
given definitions, offers its own rites of passage, and positions itself as a
divine, knowing, opposing discourse. It quite literally damns imperial pieties.
For this reason, prophets often find themselves exiled from their own communities, marked as inappropriate and impious.

Rejection from a given community due to prophetic impieties raises the
question of how prophets establish belonging to a specific discourse community to begin with. As actions, genres operate on the level of community
building and belonging. Thus, if the prophets repeatedly break genre-related
protocol, mismatch "what goes with what," and purposely choose impiety as
piety, how does the audience know they belong to *us*, or how can the critic
rightly weigh their words?

First, prophets communicate their belonging in a community by imitation of previous prophetic figures. Earlier violations of piety from prophets
become opportunities for creativity for later prophetic figures. We see such
mimesis in the call narrative of Maria Stewart in chapter 1. Stewart directly
imitates the Hebrew prophets and draws from several of them explicitly in
her narrative structure.

Second, while prophets choose form, style, and genres the audience does
not expect, they do nevertheless use forms familiar to the audience. They
live within the constraints and conventions of the community's categories
but playfully imagine how they can subvert and challenge the "'built-in'
constraints."[48] In chapter 2, for example, Richard Allen uses a "spiritual
autobiography," a well-known Puritan genre that originated with the third-
century African bishop Saint Augustine. Allen uses the genre to challenge the
authenticity of his white colleagues and establish his own authority to plant
Mother Bethel. Julia Foote, in chapter 3, also exhibits imaginative subversion
with her use of apocalyptic rhetoric in her autobiography.

Finally, prophetic figures communicate their belonging by appealing to
ideals the community holds sacred. Prophets appear when sacred ideals
seem threatened or compromised. Thus, in their impiety, they challenge the
existing pieties by appealing to the commonly held beliefs or visions. We see
Nat Turner doing this in chapter 4 as, I argue, he subverts Thomas Gray's
assumptions and appeals to a commonly held apocalyptic worldview in order
to threaten white enslavers with this-worldly divine judgment.

In its use of intertextuality, employment of unforeseen yet not foreign forms, and ideals the community holds sacred, prophetic rhetoric confronts the community's sacred language by drawing them back to a past meaning or rearranging the meaning altogether. Either way, through their impiety and inappropriateness, prophets become heretical agents to those caught within the dominant narrative. They achieve this heretical status by attacking the ideographs—the rhetorical shells of ideology that validate the hegemonic regime.

IMPLICATION NUMBER THREE:
THE PERIL OF RHETORICAL HERESY

In 1852, Frederick Douglass spoke on the Fourth of July, taking advantage of the sacredness of America's quintessential holiday. The Fourth celebrates American greatness, its pursuit of justice for all, and its independence from tyranny. After beginning his speech with a subversively tentative reference to "fellow citizens" and the use of a rhetorical question, after using prophetic reticence ("our humble offering to the national altar") and religious language "to confess . . . and express devout gratitude for the blessings," Douglass turns audience expectations on their head and denounces America for her failure to live up to her sacred ideals.

The sacred ideals of any community have verbal roots. Douglass lays out America's: *justice*, *liberty*, *prosperity*, and *independence*. He impiously denounces the ideals as "yours, not mine." The slave, Douglass famously remarks, has no stake in the Fourth of July. He refuses to allow a verbal manipulation of the Black community or the feigned ignorance of pious white America. This refusal requires a sensitivity to the specific sacred language and slogans of the American ideological community. It also requires that he risk becoming an American heretic.

By directly naming and challenging the mythological stories and slogans undergirding America, Frederick Douglass not only refuses to allow the verbal manipulation of the Black community but also commits the heresy of questioning the sacred idea of America's divine chosenness. Long before Richard T. Hughes debunked the myth of a "chosen nation,"[49] Frederick Douglass compared white Americans' concept of *chosenness*[50] with ancient Israel's election by Yahweh and rescue from Egypt:

> This, for the purpose of this celebration, is the 4th of July. It is the birthday of your National Independence, and of your political freedom. This, to you, is what the Passover was to the emancipated people

of God. It carries your minds back to the day, and to the act of your great deliverance; and to the signs, and to the wonders, associated with that act, and that day.[51]

Douglass taps into his white American audience's deepest held beliefs about national origins, moral virtue, and divine favor by citing white Americans' ideographic notion of divine election. This early, subtle reference to the myth builds the audience's confidence and expectations only for Douglass to *impiously* violate their hopes[52] and contradict their ardently believed myth. Because the Bible's notion that elect status entails an ethical obligation, Douglass scours white America with Amostic denouncement[53] and argues against the assumption of America's divine election by positing God's choice of Africa: "Africa must rise and put on her yet unwoven garment. Ethiopia shall stretch out her hand unto God."[54]

As noted, prophetic sensitivity to how language and discourses of dominance work requires an impious posture toward that which the audience deems sacred. They must criticize the verbal manipulations and slogans of oppression to subvert the idolatrous hold the ruling regime has on the oppressed community. This criticism naturally takes prophets to the verbal realm of the ideograph.

Michael Calvin McGee says ideographs operate as the verbal building blocks on which ideologies are created. Ideology "is a political language composed of slogan-like terms signifying collective commitment."[55] Ideographs (1) are ordinary terms found in political discourse which (2) use high-order abstractions to create space for illusion and misdirection. They thus represent (3) a collective commitment to a normative goal, (4) a warranted use of power, (5) and an excusing behavior that would otherwise be deemed socially or morally suspect. Still, they (6) guide or constrain behavior and belief within communal expectations and (7) are used to socialize the community toward certain political and moral ends. Further, (8) when used impiously, they become the basis for communal conviction and exile,[56] and therefore, (9) they "have the capacity to control 'power' and to influence (if not determine) the shape and texture of each individual's 'reality.'"[57] They are, in other words, the verbal construction of reality. They are the rhetorical means by which the sacredness of the oppressor's reality is reified.

These slogan-like terms thus become a prime opportunity for prophetic reimagining of reality. By questioning, criticizing, or intentionally misusing an ideograph, prophets deconstruct their power and denounce the ideology they undergird. To use religious terms, the prophet commits the heresy of impiety vis-à-vis these sacred slogans employed by the dominant regime.

Abraham J. Heschel, though not discussing ideographs, illustrates this point well: "What [prophets] attacked was, I repeat, supremely venerable: a sphere unmistakably holy; a spirituality that had both form and substance, that was concrete and inspiring, an atmosphere overwhelming the believer— pageantry, scenery, mystery, spectacle, fragrance, song, and exaltation. In the experience of such captivating sanctity, who could question the presence of God in the shape of a temple?"[58]

The prophet's job lies in the *heretical* act of criticizing what lies beyond criticism. By asking, "What if I am a woman?" Maria Stewart criticizes the ideographs and ideologies of patriarchy. Richard Allen challenges ideographs when he shoves *gospel* and *labours* together throughout his autobiography, bringing together two terms historically separated in the sacred verbal arrangements of Protestant theology. Julia Foote's elevation of herself, a woman, to messianic status challenges the sacredness of patriarchy, including Christian patriarchy. And Nat Turner calls into question the end-times theological assumptions of the white church regarding who is righteous and who is wicked.

IMPLICATION NUMBER FOUR:
RHETORIC THAT REIMAGINES THE WORLD

Because prophecy directly challenges the ideographs of a dominant community, it therefore must offer a rhetorical reframing or reimagining of reality. Herein, prophecy functions as an imaginative discourse whereby the *could be* can be an *is*. "Imagination can be thought of as reordering the objects of sense or taking them apart and imagining them in a new combination (such as centaurs) that do not themselves derive from sensory experience. It can thus become 'creative' and even visionary of things forever closed to sense."[59] Employing imaginative rearrangement and redefinitions in order to prompt thought, prophecy seeks to bring about a more just society from the embers of an oppressive one, to bring about what *could be* from the ashes of what *is*.

Concerning this dialectical tension between what *is* and what *could be* in African American women's rhetoric, Jacqueline Jones Royster and Gesa E. Kirsch note,

> While African American women's rhetorics persistently evidence their activism and advocacy of various interests, they just as persistently evidence views of hope and caring in their being, not just warriors for justice and equality but also champions of peace and prosperity as well. The discussion of either view of their performances does not

negate the other. Far from it. The existence of both views (and more) suggests instead that one view or dimension of their practices neither defines nor contains the full potential of their ways with words—any more than other examples of rhetors . . . would suggest the limits of potential for those rhetors.[60]

Trauma inhibits a community's ability to express and imagine a world outside the *is* of the oppressor's grip. When articulated from within the traumatized community, imagination becomes a powerful energizing force for the *could be*. Therefore, such world reimagining matters, particularly for communities like the Black church, who have experienced generational trauma under the dominant regime of whiteness.

Prophetic imagination, then, requires the enactment of the twofold task of the prophet: criticizing what *is* and energizing the believing community to what *could be*. Walter Brueggemann says the notion of *prophetic criticism* involves engaging in a "rejection and delegitimization of the present ordering of things," especially the delegitimization of the discourse that defines the present order.[61] This aligns with Andre E. Johnson's notions of *disputation prophecy, pessimistic prophecy*, and *judgment*.[62] Also, Robert Alter expands on this when he argues that prophets assume the role of the conscience of the people, using moral castigation and scathing critique that "oscillates between outrage against the perversion of justice, the exploitation of the poor and helpless, debauchery, and misrule, on the one hand, and cultic betrayal, the worship of pagan deities, on the other."[63]

The energizing aspect of prophecy entails the use of nurturing language that helps the alternative community imagine a *could be*, a time and situation, incongruous with the present, toward which the community can actively move.[64] It forms the audience into a community of doxology free from the numbing oppressions of their overlords. Doxology requires a new language and the "legitimization of a new rhetoric."[65] Because the prophet has already criticized the dominant discourse and its ideographs, he or she imagines and creates concrete this-worldly alternatives. As James H. Cone says, "Because trouble does not have the last word, we can fight *now* in order to realize in our present what we know to be coming in God's future."[66]

Nancy Duarte's *Resonate* examines the rhetorical structure of Martin Luther King Jr.'s prophetic "I Have a Dream" speech.[67] She demonstrates King's prophetic vacillation between what *could be* and what *is* and shows how King uses both criticism and imagination to move the audience between the now and the not yet. The prophetic denouncement of what *is* is not complete without the hopeful, energizing *could be*. Duarte's specific observation regarding King's speech also has a more universal relevance. If any piety exists in prophetic rhetoric, it exists in the fact that prophecy rarely ends in simple pessimism or escapism. Instead, it leads to hope. Even when "the prophets proclaimed Yahweh's sentence of death on Israel," they also "made known the beginnings of a new movement toward salvation."[68]

Still, calling this *piety* is difficult because the hope was uttered in an *unexpected* moment. As von Rad notes, "When the kingdom of Judah, too, had been destroyed and every political prop completely smashed, Deutero-Isaiah then delivered his message of comfort amongst those in exile, and, faced with the new situation, which he regarded as already very close at hand, broke out into jubilation which was strangely out of keeping with the dreary realities both before and after the Return."[69] In a world of despair, this hopeful imagery rarely appeals to the immediate community of prophecy but rather often transcends that audience to become an intertextual paradigm for later communities. The piety of the prophecy may not seem evident or even apply to the original hearers, but later audiences, energized by the prophetic hope, validate the prophecy. Thus, prophets often look toward the *lasting* nature of their prophecy to determine its success. This is Maria Stewart's hope as she leaves Boston and warns her audience that a prophet has been in their midst even if they did not know it. Richard Allen's autobiography also serves as reminder that the story of divine redemption continues long past the moment of audience intransigence. And Nat Turner articulates his prophetic-call narrative in a setting where he expects to die; thus, he believes the success of his words cannot be measured by the persuasion of his immediate audience.

PERILOUS PERSONAS AND PROPHESIES

Scholars readily admit "there is no universally accepted meaning for the constructed category of *prophet*."[70] However, building off Edwin Black's notion of persona,[71] Johnson helpfully provides us with the language of *prophetic persona*:

> Writers and speakers may use a persona as a rhetorical strategy because when one uses a strategy of persona, he or she assumes a character in order to "build authority" as well as "invoke cultural traditions of their audiences." One persona that is available for rhetors is that of a prophet. When a rhetor adopts a prophetic persona, he or she may attempt to do several things at once, but the primary reason is to dictate the rhetorical situation.[72]

Christopher Hobson calls this a "prophetic voice," a knowingly used style of speech and enactment the audience recognizes as prophetic.[73] Insofar as the prophet has agency, he or she utilizes an unexpected but *known* persona to assist in acquiring authority with the audience.[74]

Thus, building from the work of Johnson and Brueggemann, I define *prophetic rhetoric* as a counterimperial, ideograph-subverting message, which relies on previous rhetorical forms and a shared experience with the audience. It demands the dominant regime apply itself to the moral precepts of what the community espouses as sacred. It criticizes the dominant regime insofar as it refuses to apply itself to these standards, and it energizes the community of the oppressed to imagine and work toward what *could be*. It creates and forms its own audience by inspiring the oppressed community to long for hope and, possibly, work for revolution. It likely does not find a hearing in its original audience as it does not organize itself always for their persuasion. Still, it often finds affirmation later as the community sees the prophet's message ring true in their historical experience.[75]

LOOKING AHEAD

Through the prophetic-call narratives of Maria W. Stewart, Richard Allen, Julia Foote, and Nat Turner, we encounter the unique contributions the African American prophetic tradition makes to American oratory. These case studies—each chosen because of the diversity and unique contributions of the genre—invite us to move beyond simplistic, folkish stereotypes of nineteenth-century Black preachers to see that they employed sophisticated and thoughtful engagements with—indeed, embodiments of—the biblical text and the "text" of the world around them.

In the call narratives of Maria Stewart (chapter 1) and Julia Foote (chapter 3), we see the gendered elements that added a third layer to W. E. B. Du Bois's "double-consciousness."[76] Their stories circumvent patriarchy and resist patriarchal interpretations of the Bible through biblical, embodied, dramatic, visionary appeals that sidestep persuasion and demand either acceptance or rejection. In these chapters, we have an opportunity to see the unique contributions Black women make to our understanding of prophecy and resistance.[77]

The call narratives of Richard Allen (chapter 2) and Nat Turner (chapter 4) provide male perspectives on prophetic calling. These accounts demonstrate that call narratives are not mere historical narrations but rather occur at the dramatic intersections of racial injustices, biblical imagination, and cultural intransigence. Through Allen's use of the contradictory phrase "gospel labours" and Turner's use of apocalyptic and messianic imagery, we are invited into a rhetorical, visual world of hyperbole, contrast, cruciform, and cultural criticism that marks the Black prophetic tradition with a kind of hopeful cynicism that speaks truth regardless of its ability to persuade.

In the end, an analysis of these four call-narrative cases should generate interdisciplinary and intersectional conversation among religious studies, theology, biblical studies, African American history, ethics, psychology, sociology, political science, and rhetoric.[78] More importantly, they call on both their original audience and contemporary readers to deconstruct the *is* and imagine and enact a more equitable *could be*.

CHAPTER 1

The Call Narrative of Maria Stewart

A PROPHET LIVED AMONG YOU, AND YOU DID NOT KNOW IT

"Is this vile world a friend to grace,
To help me on to God?"

Ah, no! For it is with great tribulation that any shall enter through the gates of the holy city [Acts 14:22].

My Respected Friends, You have heard me observe that the shortness of time, the certainty of death, and the instability of all things here, induce me to turn my thoughts from earth to heaven. Borne down with a heavy load of sin and shame, my conscience filled with remorse; considering the throne of God forever guiltless, and my own eternal condemnation as just, I was at last brought to accept of salvation as a free gift, in and through the merits of a crucified Redeemer. Here I was brought to see,

'Tis not by works of righteousness
That our own hands have done,
But we are saved by grace alone,
Abounding through the Son.

After these convictions, in imagination I found myself sitting at the feet of Jesus, clothed in my right mind. For I had been like a ship tossed to and fro, in a storm at sea. Then was I glad when I realized the dangers I had escaped; and then I consecrated my soul and body, and all the powers of my mind to his service, and from that time henceforth; yea, even for evermore, amen.

I found that religion was full of benevolence; I found there was joy and peace in believing, and I felt as though I was commanded to come out from the world and be separate; to go forward and be baptized. Methought I heard a spiritual interrogation, are you able to drink of that cup that I have drank of? And to be baptized with the baptism that I have been baptized with [Matthew 20:22]? And my heart made this reply: Yea, Lord, I am able. Yet amid these bright hopes, I was filled with apprehensive fears, lest they were false. I found that sin still lurked within; it was hard for me to renounce all for Christ, when I saw my earthly prospects blasted. O, how bitter was that cup. Yet I drank it to its very dregs. It was hard for me to say, thy will be done; yet I was made to bend and kiss the rod. I was at last made willing to be anything or nothing, for my Redeemer's sake. Like many, I was anxious to retain the world in one hand, and religion in the other. "Ye cannot serve and God and mammon [Matthew 6:24]," sounded in my ear, and with giantstrength, I cut off my right hand, as it were, and plucked out my right eye, and cast them from me, thinking it better to enter life halt and maimed, rather than having two hands or eyes to be cast into hell [Mark 9:43]. Thus ended these mighty conflicts, and I received this heartcheering promise, "That neither death, nor life, nor principalities, nor powers, nor things present, nor things to come, should be able to separate me from the love of Christ Jesus, our Lord [Romans 8:38–39]."

And truly, I can say with St. Paul that at my conversion I came to the people in the fullness of the gospel of grace [Romans 15:29]. Having spent a few months in the city of———, previous, I saw the flourishing condition of their churches, and the progress they were making in their Sabbath Schools. I visited their Bible classes, and heard of the union that existed in their Female Associations. On my arrival here, not finding scarce an individual who felt interested in these subjects, and but few of the whites, except Mr. Garrison, and his friend, Mr. Knapp; and hearing that those gentlemen had observed that female influence was powerful, my soul became fired with a holy zeal for your cause; every nerve and muscle in me was engaged in your behalf. I felt that I had a great work to perform; and was in haste to make a profession of my faith in Christ, that I might be about my Father's business [Luke 2:49]. Soon after I made this profession, The Spirit of God came before me, and I said, I felt ashamed, and knew not where I should hide myself. A something said within my breast, "Press forward, I will be with thee." And my heart made this reply, Lord, if thou wilt be with me, then I will speak for thee as long as I live. And thus far I have every reason to believe that it is the divine influence of the Holy Spirit operating upon my heart that could possibly induce me to make the feeble and unworthy efforts that I have.

But to begin my subject: "Ye have heard that it hath been said, whoso is angry with his brother without a cause, shall be in danger of the judgment; and whoso shall say to his brother, Raca, shall be in danger of the council. But whosoever shall say, thou fool, shall be in danger of hellfire [Matthew 5:22]." For several years my heart was in continual sorrow. And I believe that the Almighty beheld from his holy habitation, the affliction wherewith I was afflicted, and heard the false misrepresentations wherewith I was misrepresented, and there was none to help. Then I cried unto the Lord in my troubles. And thus for wise and holy purposes, best known to himself, he has raised me in the midst of my enemies, to vindicate my wrongs before this people; and to reprove them from sin, as I have reasoned to them of righteousness and judgment to come. "For as the heavens are higher than the earth, so are his ways above our ways, and his thoughts above our thoughts [Isaiah 55:9]." I believe, that for wise and holy purposes, best known to himself, he hath unloosed my tongue, and put his word into my mouth, in order to confound and put all those to shame that have rose up against me. For he hath clothed my face with steel, and lined my forehead with brass. He hath put his testimony within me and engraved his seal on my forehead. And with these weapons I have indeed set the fiends of earth and hell at defiance.

What if I am a woman; is not the God of ancient times the God to these modern days? Did he not raise up Deborah to be a mother and judge in Israel? Did not Queen Esther save the lives of the Jews? And Mary Magdalene first declare the resurrection of Christ from the dead? Come, said the woman of Samaria, and see a man that hath told me all things that ever I did; is it not this the Christ? St. Paul declared that it was a shame for a woman to speak in public, yet our great High Priest and Advocate did not condemn the woman for a more notorious offense than this; neither will he condemn this worthless worm. The bruised reed he will not break, and the smoking flax he will not quench till he send forth judgment unto victory. Did St. Paul but know of our wrongs and deprivations, I presume he would make no objection to our pleading in public for our rights.

Again: Holy women ministered unto Christ and the apostles; and women of refinement in all ages, more or less, have had a voice in moral, religious, and political subjects. Again: Why the Almighty hath imparted unto me the power of speaking thus I cannot tell. "And Jesus lifted up his voice and said, I thank thee, O Father, Lord of heaven and earth, that thou hast hid these things from the wise and prudent and hast revealed them unworthy efforts that I have.

—MARIA W. STEWART, "WHAT IF I AM A WOMAN?," IN *LIFT EVERY VOICE: AFRICAN AMERICAN ORATORY, 1787–1900*[1]

A man possessed by a demon approached Jesus the moment he stepped off the boat in the region of the Gerasenes. For years, maybe decades, the man had skulked through the local villages naked. Instead of living in a house, he dwelt in a tomb among the dead. Regularly, the demon shackled the man entirely to its own will and drove him to utter despair and loneliness. Indeed, it so thoroughly overrode the man's will that when he spoke to Jesus, it was not his own voice but that of the demon's. Having tortured the man for many years, it now requested mercy: "Jesus, Son of God, do not torture me!"[2]

Jesus replied by requesting the demon's name. It did not, however, have a single designation. It had a title—a title not only signaling the plurality of demons within the man but also tying those demons to the dominant imperial regime in the area: Legion. The demons' name reflected the colonizing, oppressive presence of Rome. The physical colonization of the area had a felt psychological and spiritual affect.

Jesus granted Legion's request not to be tortured and instead cast them into a herd of pigs grazing on the countryside. When flushed out of the man, they rushed into the pigs, which then stampeded down the bank and drowned in the lake at the bottom.

Local farmers and merchants undoubtedly felt the immediate economic impact of the loss of their livestock. Yet when they came to confront Jesus, they found the once-possessed, once-naked, once-shackled, once-colonized man now sitting at Jesus's feet fully clothed with a lucid mind. Initially angry about their livestock, they now felt an overriding fear at the power of the one who could cast out demons and set right the mind, body, and spirit of a man they had known for decades. They asked Jesus to leave and never return. The man, however, remained as a witness to the healing power of God.

Eighteen hundred years after the events in Luke 8, Maria W. Stewart narrated her own salvation story by appealing to the story of the Gerasene demoniac and explaining that, like him, she had experienced the physical and spiritual healing of Jesus despite the dominating imperial presence of whiteness and patriarchy. Like the once-possessed man, she too sat at Jesus's feet in the posture of a disciple, fully clothed and thinking rightly. No longer shackled to the whims and logic of sin, Stewart received soteriological lucidity; no longer a ship tossed to and fro by the tides of temptation, Stewart submitted her heart, soul, mind, and strength to Christ's service. And receiving baptism, she separated herself from worldly allegiances.

The parallels, however, do not end there. Whereas the people of the region had driven Christ from their shores and whereas Christ had left the man as a living witness of God's power, Maria Stewart's typological narration shifts at this point from identification with the demon-possessed man to identification with the exiled Christ and the long history of rejected prophets.

Indeed, her narration of her salvation story served as a precursor to a more pressing saga: her prophetic-call narrative and her experience of prophetic rejection. A prophet dwelt in the midst of her audience, and they did not know it until it was too late.

As told in her speech "What If I Am a Woman?," the saga starts with a question from her Savior: "Methought I heard a spiritual interrogation, are you able to drink of that cup that I have drank of? And to be baptized with the baptism that I have been baptized with?" Without any hesitation—at least in how she narrates her calling in this last speech in Boston—she replies, "Yeah, Lord, I am able."[3] Whereas she had found the religious allure of Christ "full of benevolence" and her belief rooted in "joy and peace," Christ's question warns of crucifixion, suffering, and loneliness. Stewart will drink fully of this bitter cup. Her final speech in Boston boldly tells of that bitterness as she departs their streets as Christ departed the shores of the Gerasenes.

THE SHAPING AND SHAPE OF STEWART'S PROPHETIC RHETORIC

Indentured to a white pastor during her youth in Hartford, Connecticut, Maria W. Stewart learned the language of Christianity in childhood, affording her privileged insight that later allowed her to challenge the theologies and politics of oppression arising from white pulpits and pens. Growing up with insider social knowledge of white households and religion, she developed an awareness of white culture, biases, hypocrisies, and ignorance. She used such knowledge during her speaking career when she became the earliest woman to speak before a promiscuous audience of racial and gender-mixed hearers, breaking down both the male-female and public-private dichotomies.[4] For, indeed, "to search for women in public is to subvert a longstanding tenet of the modern Western gender system, the presumption that social space is divided between the public and the private and that men claim the former while women are confined to the latter."[5] Thus, the experience of being a Black woman around whiteness likely molded her views on gender oppression and her belief that Black women's labor was designed to hinder their achievement of education and social power.[6]

Still, Stewart did not lack education or skills in social suasion. Marilyn Richardson refers to her as "America's first Black woman political writer."[7] No woman before Stewart had grappled, as she did, "with the intersectionalities of being American, African, and a woman on a public platform."[8] Her political insights thus "served as the catalyst for production of numerous treatises on the black experience up to the Civil War."[9] However, as already indicated, while the political elements in Stewart's writing and speaking merit consideration, Stewart also adopted a prophetic persona that surpassed mere politics and thoughtfully subverted the Enlightenment binaries of her white nineteenth-century contemporaries with their bifurcation of religious and political thought. As Valerie C. Cooper notes, "Although her work has been widely categorized as political speech, it also rings with evangelical religious fervor because it is liberally sprinkled with biblical references. . . . Modern binaries of sacred versus secular (or even church versus state) are not relevant to Stewart, who acknowledges no such divisions in her writing."[10] We cannot, then, separate Stewart's religious or prophetic message from her political philosophies, radical ideals, or gender egalitarianism. Indeed, the combination of her political ideals and religious convictions generated the prophetic, rhetorical impieties that violated audience expectations. "Although black and white women were generally accepted as evangelists, preachers, and missionaries in most church denominations by the early nineteenth century, they were not expected to speak publicly on political matters."[11] The public nature of Stewart's prophetic impieties had massive implications for a Black woman already vulnerable to racist and gendered accusations of insanity.

> Women were labeled "mad," "insane," "unwomanly," or "unnatural," for actions considered unmotherly, selfish, willful, violent, or overtly sexual. This label even extended to women who demanded such things as equality, a college education, the right to vote, or a job outside the home. . . . [A] study in the leading psychological journal of its day argued that freedom caused mental illness in African Americans. This logic emerged from proslavery, racist arguments,

which insisted that slavery civilized African Americans, and once freed, they degenerated into their "natural" states of depravity, immorality, and even mental illness.[12]

The dominant regime must question prophets' sanity because the prophets' disinterest in conforming to the false narratives and ideologies of the ruling class. However, the charges against their sanity require, then, that prophetic figures, especially female ones, find ways to justify their calling. Stewart's call narration illustrates this effort.

The irony of Maria W. Stewart relaying her call narrative in her speech "What If I Am a Woman?" lies in the fact that the speech is a farewell address.[13] This was her farewell before she left public life and Boston altogether and moved to New York to become a teacher. In theory, she had nothing to lose and nothing to justify in this speech. She could have raged against her enemies or lamented the slowness of the justice process. Kristin Waters, however, says the speech abandons "the travails of the past" and "emanates hope."[14] Stewart had earlier lamented the attacks of her interlocutors, the financial and social attacks of her enemies, the malicious misrepresentations of her personhood, and the struggles and slowness of her antislavery work in Boston. But in this speech, delivered in a schoolroom of the African Meeting House in Boston, Massachusetts, in 1833, she expressed "less of the bitterness found in her earlier thought."[15]

Cooper, however, argues that Stewart's disposition in the speech was as aggressive as ever. It resounded with prophetic intensity and a lack of interest in persuasion. "Gone are the coy facades; in their place, she makes a bold case for the rights of women."[16] Cooper notes how, in earlier speeches, she demurred or expressed reticence. However, in this speech, Stewart *intensified* her calling and its demands by removing her experiences from *human* time and placing them in heavenly time, associating herself more with Jesus than David Walker and expressing no reticence. She wanted her hearers to understand the opportunity they had missed. A prophet had lived among them, and they did not know it. Linking "her philosophy of everyday righteousness and political struggle together with an apocalyptic justice,"[17] Stewart's farewell speech countered the racists and sexist arguments for Black and female inferiority by highlighting the achievements of both the continent of Africa and female intellectuals. Still, the combination of such diverse yet intersected interests, particularly infused as they are with religion, marks Stewart's prophetic intentions and justifies her calling.

To see how these elements work together, we must understand the moral implications of call narratives, Stewart's resistance of the cult of true womanhood, the structural intentionality of call narratives, and the way the Black church has historically used such narratives for liberative purposes.

NARRATIVE AND MORAL PARTICIPATION

The first observation about prophetic-call narratives is that they are narratives, "symbolic actions—words and/or deeds—that have sequence and meaning for those who live, create, or interpret them."[18] Call narratives, like narratives in general, challenge "the notions that human communication— if it is to be considered rhetorical—must be an argumentative form, that reason is to be attributed only to discourse marked by clearly identifiable modes of inference and/or implication, and that the norms for evaluation of rhetorical communication must be rational standards taken essentially from informed or formal logic."[19] One benefit of narrative lies in its ability to foster public moral discourse without resorting to mere syllogisms. Narration, particularly within the prophetic traditions, is a meaning-making social action. It gathers hearers into a counterlogic or alternative mythology that rethinks political engagement and paths toward "resolving the problems of public moral argument."[20]

Thomas Hoyt Jr. says the Black rhetorics of resistance have relied heavily on narration because "by telling a story, one could create or destroy a world view."[21] Narrative invites the audience to participate in this creation or destruction. Whereas traditional Aristotelian reason renders the audience—as nonexperts—irrational, narration renders the audience capable of moral judgments and thus as moral participants and cocreators of the narrative and the new world it imagines. In prophetic narratives, the audience thus learns the morally loaded language and methods of resistance to an oppressive, dominant consciousness. In call narratives, they are swept into an origins story that they must accept or reject at the outset.

CALL NARRATIVE AS THESIS STATEMENT

Audience acceptance or rejection of a call narrative does not require of them a decision before they are ready because call narratives operate as narrative theses, both justifying the prophet and embodying the details of their ministry of rhetoric. The objective of the narrative therefore lies specifically in inviting the hearer to participate in—and understand the implications of—the moral, religious, and political consequences of the story.[22] Much therefore hangs on the audience's perception of the call narrative, particularly when they are skeptical.

Audience skepticism of call narration matters most to Black women, who have had to justify their prophetic calling and assert their prophetic theses in the face of patriarchal disbelief. We saw this in the call narrative of Jarena Lee in the introduction when Lee described the divine impulse to interrupt Reverend Williams and finish his sermon.[23] Kimberly P. Johnson says, "By speaking up, Lee crossed the divide between the private and public domains. She stepped out of her assigned private domain to take on the preaching role (reserved for men) in the public domain."[24] Lee thus uses this story to justify her calling in a way that Richard Allen could not deny:

> I now sat down, scarcely knowing what I had done, being frightened. I imagined that for this indecorum, as I feared it might be called, I should be expelled from the church. But instead of this, the Bishop [Richard Allen] rose up in the assembly, and related that I had called upon him eight years before, asking to be permitted to preach, and that he had put me off; but that he now as much believed that I was called to that work, as any of the preachers present.[25]

Lee's narrative both justifies her calling and "serves as a public indictment against the early African Methodist Episcopal (AME) Church for marginalizing women by not allowing female ministers to serve in the denomination."[26] This justificatory element demonstrates the thesis-like role the call narrative performs.

To say the call narrative in the African American prophetic tradition takes on a thesis-like role for the prophet does not merely explicate *that* the prophet is called to prophetic ministry but also *why* and to *what end*. It functions as a piece of the political and prophetic paradigm for ministry establishing the prophet's authority, challenging the oppressor's authority, and reenvisioning the world according to a different set of moral possibilities. Thus, the prophet's call, like the prophet's message, does not merely state the facts of what *is* but inspires hope by reimagining the world as it *could be*.

THE CULT OF TRUE WOMANHOOD

The call narratives of women specifically supersede the gender qualifications because such narratives summon forth the seed of egalitarianism within the Christian tradition.[27] Maria W. Stewart's call narrative demonstrates her belief, along with her prophetess counterparts throughout history, that the God self-disclosed to the world of men has also self-disclosed to women. Indeed, if all persons have succumbed to Adam's sin, then the daughters of Eve ought not to be silenced more than any man. In this reasoning, the same arguments that worked for racial equality could also find employment within the fight for gender equality because their rootedness in the biblical text and its logic. Through an egalitarian biblical hermeneutic and by means of the authority bestowed in her call narrative, Stewart's prophetic thesis lays the axe of prophetic utterance to the roots of the trees of patriarchy and prejudice, making her "instrumental in shaping a tradition in which women authorize themselves as speaking subjects by adapting apocalyptic rhetoric of Protestant ministerial traditions and combining it with repeated calls for compassion and mercy."[28] Not everyone, however, saw prophecy against patriarchy and prejudice as palatable.

To understand the gendered rhetorical situation of Stewart and other nineteenth-century Black women, we must appreciate the cult of true womanhood, or the cult of domesticity. Though a phrase coined by later historians, the cult of true womanhood arose from the intersection of eighteenth- and nineteenth-century Christianity, patriarchal gender roles, racial prejudice, and sexual identity in middle-class Western Europe. Beth Allision Barr notes three cultural roots of the cult of true womanhood: (1) biological essentialism—that is, the Enlightenment's notions of sex difference and its inherent bifurcation of public and private; (2) early modern science that argued that women were genetically weaker than men and biologically akin to children; and (3) the Industrial Revolution, which separated the domestic space from the workspace and, with the Enlightenment binaries, divided the public and private.[29]

"True womanhood" functioned as a kind of socioeconomic and religious means of constraining the ethics, particularly the sexual ethics, of white women and limiting their access to public civic power. While the cult held so much social sway that "it cut across class and national borders affecting peasant women and queens,"[30] class privilege and racial hierarchy became its defining markers as peasant women and Black women had neither the means nor the opportunity to fulfill the requirements of "true womanhood." In other words, Black women were de facto not *women*, and intersectional oppressive forces ensured they stayed that way.

This omission of poor and Black women from the category of *women* did not occur by accident. Valerie Cooper argues, "Implicit in the Cult of True Womanhood was the supposition that white women were its fullest, highest expression."[31] The cult of true womanhood's racism and classism allowed social elites to define their own piety, purity, domesticity, and therefore *womanhood* over against Black women and poor women (whether white or Black). Thus, it "demonized prostitutes, working girls, and dance halls, elevating the home as the safest place for respectable women."[32]

Even privileged white women experienced demonization when they ventured out of the private sphere and spoke in public about politics. Phyliss M. Japp highlights this in Angelina Grimke's abolitionist speeches: "The problem scarcely seemed critical at first, when [Angelina Grimke's] listeners consisted of women gathered in private parlors. The situation quickly changed, however, when men began attending the women's gatherings and crowds grew too large for private homes. Angelina soon found herself addressing mixed audiences in public lecture halls. In these situations, her gender was the decisive factor in audience response."[33] Going public in her speeches challenged male-female *and* public-private binaries constraining nineteenth-century women. Thus, Grimke adopted a prophetic persona; drawing off the Hebrew prophets, "she assumed a forceful, dynamic, 'male' posture."[34]

Given that even white women speaking in public challenged patriarchal binaries, Black women posed an even greater threat as they a priori challenged male-female, white-Black, and wealthy-poor binaries and thereby "subverted these idealized race and gender roles . . . in their efforts to create and project alternative identities for themselves."[35] Jamie L. Carlacio highlights the subversive nature of this saying: "Stewart exposed 'true' womanhood as a racist and classist metaphor designed to exclude all but middle-class white women" by asserting her rights as a woman, a public intellectual, and a prophetic figure.[36] Carlacio continues, in her "Address Delivered to the African-American Female Intelligence Society of America," Stewart argues for her right, as a Black woman, to speak in public and elevate the status of Black women by extending "the meaning of 'true' womanhood to include . . . African American women. She has taken the terms of the dominant culture and metaphorically turned them into terms that describe all women, regardless of race or class. Stewart has thus ostensibly destabilized the category of 'women' so that any woman might conceivably hold power and influence not only within her family but also within her community."[37] Thus, Black women speaking in public threatened all the binaries of the Enlightenment's gender essentialism. By noting the prophetic impieties in her speech "What If I Am a Woman?," we see Stewart's undeniable wrestling with the gender constraints in the cult of true womanhood and its false binaries.

MEN, WOMEN, AND THE PUBLIC CHARACTER
OF PROPHETIC CALLING

At the time they receive their call, men already have varying degrees of access to the public sphere. The divine order of the creation, patriarchy assumes, has given men the right to arrange the public political elements of society. Receiving a call may propel them further into the public, but from the beginning, their privilege provides access to spaces traditionally denied to women.

Call narratives thus become a means by which women legitimize not only their message and ministry but also the very fact of going public. Given that Black women's "public activities were circumscribed by the actions of black men . . . [with] black men somehow [having] to sanction women's efforts in order for their voices to have public meaning,"[38] the questions, concerns, and calling to go public remain uniquely female experiences. Black women who have received the call must both criticize white racial patriarchy and Black gendered patriarchy. More, they must deconstruct the alleged divine sanctioning of both. Women like Maria Stewart must articulate their callings in ways that preempt accusations of attacking the divine order of creation: white over Black, men over women.

Even if she can gain a hearing beyond these accusations, she then enters a rhetorical arena where masculine norms dictate her reception. James Darsey outlines three significant ways American radical rhetoric and Old Testament prophesy intersect: "Both have in common a sense of mission, a desire to bring the practice of people into accord with a sacred principle, and an uncompromising, often excoriating stance toward a reluctant audience."[39] With each of these, we can see the potential and real conflict female prophets may experience. First, while Black men and women may find a mutual mission in racial liberation, the female mission includes liberation from gendered patriarchy. Second, while Black men and women both share the desire to bring the practice of whites and Black people into accord with sacred principles, they do not always agree on what that sacred principle *means*. For both, the theological principle of one God having created all the races serves as the umbrella under which white and Black folks find liberation from injustice, but Black women uniquely have to justify speaking that sacred principle in public. Finally, whereas Black men must have an uncompromising stance in relation to an audience that is reluctant regarding (1) their Logos and (2) their race, Black women have a third component added to this reluctance: their sex, which implicitly calls into question their Logos, ethos, and pathos all at the same time. Thus, even the reluctance of the audience takes on unique features in relation to female prophets.

One specific way the audience's reluctance assumes male norms and is therefore suspicious of female prophets has to do with the patriarchal characteristics associated with prophetic figures, which involve narratives of "extraordinary (re)birth or conversion," often including "extraordinary vision, comparable to the visions of the Old Testament prophets."[40] Additionally, the receiver gets imbued with *charism* and *charisma* that the community must receive and recognize. However, what the community considers a pragmatically valuable charism and what suffices as a rhetorically effective charisma get largely defined by male expressions. The female prophet's charisms and charisma undoubtedly look different—especially when any loss of emotional or physical control only furthers stereotypes—and therefore she receives harsher judgment than her male counterparts within in the context of the cult of true womanhood.[41]

Yet aside from her disposition and rhetorical strategies, her use of the Bible resonated most effectively with her audience. Against contemporary progressive expectations, Stewart employed the Bible to subvert patriarchal norms and justify her public prophetic calling. The rest of this chapter explores how her use of specific scriptures in her call narrative work together to subvert racial and gender patriarchies.

GENRE, CHARACTER, AND STRUCTURE OF CALL NARRATIVES

African American prophetic-call narratives, like Maria Stewart's, intertextually renarrate the call narratives of the biblical prophets specifically by mimicking the cadence, content, and structure of their biblical precursors. Their objective lies in providing a thesis statement for further prophetic utterance and thus a justification for all prophetic acts. "The call commissioned the prophet: the act of writing down an account of it was aimed at those sections of the public in whose eyes he had to justify himself."[42] Consequently, prophetic-call narratives, like the larger genre of prophetic rhetoric, function as a rhetoric of intense moral conflict, especially when women receive the calling. It would be surprising indeed "if distinctive stylistic features did not appear as strategic adaptations to a difficult rhetorical situation."[43] After all, the prophetic-call narrative, like all genres, exists in "dynamic responsiveness to situational demands."[44] Call narratives imply God-given authority and verify the prophet's merits to carry the mantle and communicate the message. The weight of such a task, it turns out, may explain why call narratives have such a consistent structure. Thus, to appreciate Stewart's narrative, we must understand the structures she employs.

CALL-NARRATIVE STRUCTURE

Because Maria Stewart "contended that the Bible spoke to her and of her, and she employed a hermeneutic that privileged as its interpretive key her identity as an African American and as a woman,"[45] it is helpful to see her call narrative in light of the call narratives of the Hebrew prophets. Such narratives are structured in repeated, familiar ways that force the audience to evaluate the prophet's authenticity. While the biblical text has a diversity of prophetic-call narratives, Norm Habel accurately draws out six structural elements that occur most frequently: "(1) the divine confrontation; (2) the introductory word; (3) the commission; (4) the objection; (5) the reassurance; and (6) the sign."[46]

Because using these familiar structural elements assists prophetic credibility and authority, we should not be surprised that Black women utilized them to justify their callings.[47] After all, the use of predictable elements demonstrates that the prophet understands audience language and values, even as he or she intends to subvert audience expectations.[48] We see all this in play in Maria Stewart's call narrative, which displays the following aspects: (1) Yahweh confronts the individual; (2) an introductory word is given; (3) God commissions the prophet; (4) the male prophets object; Stewart does not; (5) divine assurance is given; and (6) a sign of divine presence and empowerment appears. Like her male counterparts, Stewart appeals to the Hebrew prophets in her call narrative. The more closely she can bring her story into the biblical framework, the more she forces her listeners to recognize her divine authority.

YAHWEH CONFRONTS THE (WO)MAN

In contrast to a number of biblical accounts of divine calling where God appears through a divine messenger (Judges 6:12) or a mediating object (Exodus 3) and in contrast to certain prophets who receive direct visions of God (Isaiah 6; Ezekiel 1), God's confrontation with Maria Stewart occurs through divine utterance, like that of Jeremiah (Jeremiah 1:5). God confronts her with a creative word that establishes new possibilities of liberation. This word Stewart hears, however, does not come in the form of bold declarations of prenatal choice, but rather comes in the form of questions: "Methinks I heard a spiritual interrogation—'Who shall go forward, and take off the reproach that is cast upon the people of color? Shall it be a woman?'" and "Me thought I heard a spiritual interrogation, are you able to drink of that cup that I have drank of?[49]

The Hebrew prophets received their divine callings at specific, intentional times (*kairos*) in the history of Israel: the precise moment when their voice—or God's voice through them—was needed most or was most disruptive to the dominant consciousness. This disruption occurs, in language provided by narrative criticism, as a disruption of the accepted mode of being. This is why "call narratives do not reside exclusively within an ecclesial context. Folks are pushed, pulled, prodded, and picked at in many ways to do things that they did not think they would ever do or to serve in ways they could not previously imagine."[50] Everyday life is disrupted via extraordinary, extrasensory visions, voices, and experiences.

This disruptive divine word to a Black woman arrived in a climactic moment through a seemingly anticlimactic person, a nonperson whose voice threw the social order into disarray. "In claiming that she was called by God, Stewart unsettles the patriarchal order by contending that God is imbuing a woman with the authority to act on his behalf. What was once the entitlement of men is now the privilege of a woman, and a black woman no less."[51] Prophetic-call narratives democratize authority and power beyond the boundaries of gender.

Due to the cult of true womanhood's social power, rhetorics and rituals of power would have constantly reminded a woman like Stewart that she was designed by God for the domestic sphere, lacking the intellectual ability or emotional stability to speak publicly. The call narrative, however, disrupts even these supposedly divine orderings of life. "The call marks the initial interruption of God in the life of the individual. Such a moment was related as a supernatural confrontation which could be comprehended with the senses and tested by rational dialogue."[52] Rational dialogue, contrasted with the stereotypes of an irrational and emotional womanhood, drives Stewart's call story. Prior to the divine encounter, she felt *more* unstable: "For I had been like a ship tossed to and fro,[53] in a storm at sea."[54] The prophetic call, however, aligns her mind to reason and divinity: "After these convictions I found myself siting at the feet of Jesus, clothed and in my right mind. . . ."[55] Then was I glad when I realized the dangers I had escaped; and then I consecrated my soul and body, and all the powers of my mind to his service."[56]

The divine confrontation brings about the most reasonable circumstances whereby Stewart sees herself as a student at the feet of Jesus and a vessel for his words. In this narrative move, Stewart self-legitimizes her authority as a prophet: "Stewart's credibility as a speaker is predicated not simply on the authority of her mind but on a divine power that animates her soul and bolsters the veracity of her words. . . . If [the audience finds] Stewart's critiques offensive and her style unladylike, then they place themselves in direct opposition to

God's will."[57] To deny her divine calling, one must demonstrate not only that she is irrational but also that she has invented the story of her calling.

AN INTRODUCTORY WORD IS GIVEN

The specifics of God's message also matter to Stewart's call narrative. She earlier described God's introductory word as a "divine interrogation" whereby God asks both about her ability to drink the cup of suffering and her willingness to take the reproach off the divine community. In the Hebrew prophetic tradition, this call through interrogation is best known in the prophet Isaiah call narrative in Isaiah 6: "Whom shall I send? And who shall go for us?"[58] The question comes on the heels of Isaiah's temple vision wherein he sees God "sitting on a throne, high and lofty, and the hem of his robe filled the temple."[59] Further, Isaiah's calling also happens in the *kairos* moment of King Uzziah's death (Isaiah 6:1). When the earthly king dies, Isaiah sees the heavenly king enthroned. If Stewart relies on Isaiah for her introductory interrogation, she likely aims to foreshadow divine judgment wherein earthly structures of power and security get revealed as limited and mortal in the presence of the speaking God who sits sovereignly on his throne. This introductory interrogation, then, functions as an explanation and preparation—a thesis for her prophetic ministry.[60]

I should note, however, that calling via divine commandment does not feature prominently in African American prophetic-call narratives despite its frequency in biblical call narratives. Hobson suggests this may have to do with the generally accepted belief that "God's direct authorization of prophecy had ceased after the canonical prophets."[61] While Stewart may have also agreed with such a statement, she saw her "spiritual interrogation" as nothing less than a command in the form of a question. Whereas humans may question their calling for racial, gendered, or theological reasons, God has already questioned her in a way that supersedes theirs: "Shall it be a woman?"

YAHWEH COMMISSIONS THE (WO)MAN

Isaiah's interrogation is not the only scripture she cites. God's question of her willingness to "take off the reproach" of his people also communicates her commission as it intertextually references the book of Ezekiel: "Neither will I cause men to hear in thee the shame of the heathen any more, neither shalt thou bear the reproach of the people any more, neither shalt thou cause thy nations to fall any more, saith the Lord GOD."[62] Ezekiel's larger context presents a prophetic warning against Edom and other nations that have devoured and enslaved the people of Israel. The prophecy also, however, provides hope for Israel because the people are told they will no longer bear the weight of shameful subordination to such nations. By employing the Ezekiel prophesy in her call narrative, Stewart recognizes the dangers of her call to speak against the oppressive nation but also conveys that her hearing of the "words from elsewhere" authorizes her as a voice of liberation and hope for Black people—God's chosen people. The two callings are intertwined and inseparable, reflective of the general structure of both the Hebrew prophetic tradition and the African American jeremiad.[63]

Still, even here, we must consider the gender issues. No one would have objected to a woman speaking a word of encouragement to an oppressed people. But a public word of indictment against an oppressive political entity like a nation was considered a distinctively male domain. Apocalyptic fervor and militancy may have been appropriate for David Walker but inappropriate for Maria Stewart. Nevertheless, as the thesis statement of a prophetic ministry that later employed violent and militant rhetoric in her condemnation of white power, Stewart's call narrative relies heavily on this Ezekiel passage of warning to the nations and hope for Israel. In this, we see

> Stewart's Christianity is far from the compassionate and domesticated religion modern readers often associated with the nineteenth-century woman's sphere. Indeed, from the beginning of her public discourse, the vengeance/love–male/female dichotomies were disrupted by Stewart. The ferocity and militarism in Stewart's language refuse antebellum compulsory norms requiring female discourse to be properly 'feminine'; that is, to avoid the kinds of topics and rhetorical modes that Stewart marshals in her lectures.[64]

Again, Stewart refuses to succumb to the false binaries so dominant in white, patriarchal religion. We can add secular-sacred and public-private dichotomies to the list as well.

THE *MAN* OBJECTS; THE (WO)MAN DOES NOT

When God calls the prophet Isaiah, he replies that his lips are too unclean to proclaim God's message. When Jeremiah experiences his calling, he argues that his youth should disqualify him. Ezekiel conveys a feeling of deep distress after he receives his calling. Jonah outright flees to the other side of the world after receiving his call to preach to Nineveh. Throughout the Bible, prophetic figures respond with reticence to God's initial calling. The frequency of this narrative element suggests that only false prophets *want* the task.

The predictable objection of male Hebrew prophets when called on by God provides us with our most significant opportunity to see Stewart's break from patriarchal norms. Reticence has a specific function for Black women, who have to show it in order to avoid appearing as if they intentionally chose a masculine role. Seeking prophetic power might lead to, as Raymie McKerrow notes, "the ultimate act of excommunicating those who fail to participate in or accede to the rituals" of patriarchal power: "The social structures of discourse . . . begin with '*restrictions* on who may speak, how much may be said, what may be talked about, and on what occasion.' These restrictions are more than socially derived regulators of discourse; they are institutionalized rules accepted and used by the dominant class to control the discursive actions of the dominated."[65] Thus, reticence has pragmatic benefit to prophets generally but specifically to female prophets because they challenge the gendered "world of 'taken-for-granted' discourse," which generally shields itself from question and criticism "by accepting only certain individuals as the authorities who can speak."[66]

Yet whereas the Hebrew prophets might say, "Ah! Lord God! Behold, I cannot speak: for I am a child" or "Who am I [to do such a task]?"[67] Mariah Stewart's response to her spiritual interrogation, oddly, conveys no objection. William H. Myers observes that women, even within denominations that have female preachers, still feel "great internal conflict because of their gender" such that they argue with God over their calling.[68] Stewart's lack of reticence and resistance also strikes me as odd not only because of the pragmatic rhetorical benefits of narrating reticence but also because Stewart makes frequent use of reticence and hesitancy in other places, including in other narrations of her call narrative. Shirley Wilson Logan observes that Maria Stewart regularly employs rhetorical insinuation—"a rhetorical move wherein the speaker claims her inadequacy or lack of qualifications for the task and asks the audience's indulgence. A way of ingratiating oneself with the audience, *insinuatio* allows the speaker to acquire the auditors' initial goodwill and support. It was clearly an essential move for a black woman speaking publicly in 1832."[69] Here, however, in her call narrative in "What If I Am a Woman?," she goes out of her way to indicate her willingness to accept the mantle of the prophet. Why?

Her lack of reticence, her overt willingness, comes out most clearly in "What If I Am a Woman?" when she narrates God's interrogation of her, "Are you able to drink of that cup that I have drank of?" It is tempting to see this as a reference to the garden of Gethsemane, where Jesus prays and asks God to remove "this cup" of suffering (the cross) from him.[70] But the reference to "the cup that I have drank" occurs in question form for a specific reason—it highlights a question Jesus asked James and John in the book of Matthew to emphasize their desire for power without suffering:

> Then came to him the mother of Zebedees children with her sons, worshipping him, and desiring a certain thing of him. And he said unto her, What wilt thou? She saith unto him, Grant that these my two sons may sit, the one on thy right hand, and the other on the left, in thy kingdom. But Jesus answered and said, Ye know not what ye ask. Are ye able to drink of the cup that I shall drink of, and to be baptized with the baptism that I am baptized with? They say unto him, We are able. And he saith unto them, Ye shall drink indeed of my cup, and be baptized with the baptism that I am baptized with: but to sit on my right hand, and on my left, is not mine to give, but it shall be given to them for whom it is prepared of my Father. And when the ten heard it, they were moved with indignation against the two brethren. But Jesus called them unto him, and said, Ye know that the princes of the Gentiles exercise dominion over them, and they that are great exercise authority upon them. But it shall not be so among you: but whosoever will be great among you, let him be your minister; And whosoever will be chief among you, let him be your servant: Even as the Son of man came not to be ministered unto, but to minister, and to give his life a ransom for many.[71]

Stewart's call story cites this scripture for several subversive reasons. First, the text climaxes with an egalitarian leadership structure that reflects nothing else seen in the world.[72] It imagines a kingdom so radically egalitarian that the greatest in the kingdom become the servants and the servants become the greatest. Stewart's prophetic calling imagines and longs for such a world.

Second, in this text, jealousy circulates among the disciples regarding the potential positioning of James and John.[73] Jesus clarifies that he has no authority to grant the position these two seek; thus, the other disciples should not experience jealousy over it, especially because this call leads to suffering, not glory. So, too, Maria Stewart wants to contend that her calling does not lead to glory, but suffering. Her brothers in the faith have no reason to feel threatened by her call to prophetic suffering.

Third, and most importantly, Stewart cites this text because it shows the utter failure of the male disciples of Jesus to prepare for enduring such suffering. When Jesus asks James and John, "Can ye drink of the cup that I drink of?" he implies a negative answer: "Ye know not what ye ask." These two inner-circle disciples of Jesus seek the glory of Jesus's kingdom but cannot endure its cup of suffering. But this is not so for Stewart. God has no implied negative answer to the question. And she offers no objection or resistance to the calling: "Yeah, Lord, I am able." Whereas Jesus indicts James and John (and by implication, many male prophetic figures around Stewart) for their inability to endure suffering, Stewart aligns herself with Jesus in Gethsemane (now she shifts scenes to contrast herself with James and John more explicitly) when she says, "If it be thy will be it even so, Lord Jesus!"[74] Just as Jesus in the garden asks for a removal of the cup of suffering yet ultimately also says, "Not my will, but thine be done,"[75] so, too, Stewart offers her will up to God. She seeks no personal glory. She knows this road ends in suffering. As a Black woman, she has experienced enduring this road in a way that Black men only know the half of and white women only know the other half of.

Stewart's citation of Matthew 20 possibly contains the most subversive element of her prophetic-call narrative. Within it, she shows the egalitarian leadership structure of the kingdom of God, chastises her male naysayers by calling out their jealousy, and aligns herself with Jesus in Gethsemane in contrast to her male counterparts who align themselves with the power-hungry, bickering disciples, who knew nothing of the true selfless cost of their calling. Herein she "not only indicates her divine calling to act in public but also implicitly critiqued black men for their failure to act courageously on behalf of black people."[76] Stewart refuses to express reticence about her calling; in this last public speech she ever makes, she refuses to allow the audience to think they encountered anyone less than a prophet in their midst.

DIVINE REASSURANCE IS GIVEN

Still, while Stewart says, "I am able" to endure the cup of suffering, she still needs reassurance. The Christian tradition reminds her of her finitude: "I found that sin still lurked within; it was hard for me to renounce all for Christ, when I saw my earthly prospects blasted."[77] Despite her boldness, she struggles not with her ability to endure the suffering, but with the residue of sin: "It was hard for me to say, thy will be done."[78]

God sovereignly steps into anxiousness, and "I was made to bend and kiss the rod."[79] "Kiss the rod" is Shakespearean phrase referring to submitting to one's superior. Nevertheless, Stewart seems to be making a biblical reference with it as it parallels her statement "I was at last willing to be anything or nothing, for my Redeemer's sake."[80] God had apparently taught her obedience and submission. God had prepared her to drink of the cup of suffering. In this, she moves from anxiety to assurance. She realizes, unlike James and John, that she cannot serve two masters,[81] and her devotion now extends so far that she prepares to endure all the personal discipline required of a good disciple in the Sermon on the Mount, including maiming her vision or severing appendages if necessary. This single-mindedness becomes the causal factor in her reassurance: "Thus ended my many mighty conflicts."[82] She sits in biblical Sabbath, enjoys a time of Jubilee, and inhabits in a period of peace of the sort depicted in Judges after a long struggle with disobedience.

We can appreciate the significance of divine affirmation for Stewart and other women only when seen in the larger context. One observation I make in chapter 2 when discussing Richard Allen's call narrative is that men's experiences of prophetic calling tend to have less dramatic flair. The reason for this lies in the fact that their stories are more frequent and less scrutinized. As men, they do not have to endure the same level of skepticism as women. Thus, "divine validation is in some sense more important for women because they don't receive the same quantity or quality of human validation as men do."[83] A powerful moment of assurance from God goes a long way to easing Stewart's anxiety and, more importantly for the narrative, assuring her skeptical hearers.

A SIGN OF DIVINE PRESENCE AND EMPOWERMENT

Whereas the Hebrew prophets often receive powerful signs indicating the presence of the divine when sent out to prophesy, Stewart's call narrative conveys a more subtle, but no less potent, sign of God's presence. After asserting her wrestling, she finally states, "Thus ended my many conflicts, and I received this heart-cheering promise: That neither death, nor life, nor principalities, nor powers, nor things present, nor things to come, should be able to separate me from the love of Christ Jesus, our Lord," referring to Romans 8:38–39.[84] Her citation of the apostle Paul here provides a unique insight into her hermeneutic and call narration, particularly because of Paul's association with patriarchy.

Monika R. Alston-Miller problematizes the way scholars have understood Stewart's self-identification. Rather than merely sweeping away Pauline imperatives, as many feminists have, Stewart adopts a liminal position, a "space between the boundaries of religious and civic discourse"[85] by fusing traditionally masculine voices (e.g., preachers) with traditionally feminine roles (e.g., spiritual mother and social reformer).

This breakdown or fusing of gender binaries, however, only scratches the surface of Stewart's subtlety and subversion. In her engagement of Paul, she references his various texts and positions herself as an embodiment of Paul's vision for pastoral, prophetic figures in the church. First, she further directly associates herself with him as the founder of Christianity when she says, "and truly, I can say with St. Paul . . ."[86] Second, she responds in the same way the apostles did to the inspiration of the Holy Spirit.[87] Thus, she establishes that in what follows, she has no intention of contradicting Paul. How, then, can she claim the role of overseer in the church and teacher of the Bible when Paul seems to have restricted those roles to men?[88] Stewart answers that the apostle Paul would change his mind about the public role of women if he had seen Black women's suffering.[89] She neither disagrees with Paul nor suggests her adversaries have misunderstood him. She says, rather, that his comments remain irrelevant because his writings did not address her rhetorical situation. Thus, she understands herself not only as a faithful exegete of what Paul has said but also as a faithful exegete of what Paul *would say* if he understood the contemporary context under which Black women suffer.

To understand the force of Stewart's citation of Paul's well-known text from Romans 8, we should notice Stewart's subtle pronoun shift. Paul does not say, "should be able to separate *me* from the love of Christ Jesus," but rather Paul says, "should be able to separate *us* from the love of Christ Jesus." Stewart says this text served as a "heart-cheering promise" that she specifically received from God. For her, this text does not merely function as a general announcement to the church as whole regarding God's presence but also as a divine affirmation that no loss of life, property, spiritual force, or human criticism can stay God's divine, protective presence. The sign of God's abiding presence appears as nothing less than a personalized scripture God gives directly to Maria Stewart, which provides a "sense of relief that the burden that came with the call experience and continued, even heightened, during the struggle is now lifted."[90]

The citation of a Pauline text transitions Stewart to her final indicator of divine presence and legitimization of her prophetic call. Part of what Stewart needs to do to legitimize her ministry as a prophetic woman before the church necessitates navigating those problematic patriarchal texts from the Pauline corpus. Stewart's ability to work with and reinterpret Paul—the writer of two-thirds of the New Testament and a man who himself experienced a dramatic call from Christ—proves a necessary piece of going public with her prophetic ministry and demonstrating God's presence with her.

Stewart traverses this Pauline topography not by tackling it head-on or explaining away Pauline household codes, but by reimagining herself as the new Paul. "And truly, I can say with St. Paul that at my conversion I came to the people in the fullness of the gospel of grace."[91] From here, she mentions her stay in a certain unnamed city, the flourishing conditions of churches, the progress of schools, her visitation of Bible courses, and her hearing of a certain female leader of a female association. She also references a disinterested audience upon her arrival (aside from Mr. Garrison), who later observed the power of her female influence, which sparked a holy zeal for her audience. Soon thereafter, the Spirit of God came upon her, and she spoke before many people.[92]

The key observation to make in this final section of her call narrative is her mimicking of Paul's narrative pacing. Just as Jesus reenacted the story of Moses in Matthew 1–5, so Maria Stewart reenacts the traveling narrative and concerns of Saint Paul. Her explicit citation of Romans 15:9 is followed by a rhythmic reciting of Paul's travels throughout the rest of Romans 15, only they are filled with Stewart's travels and experiences. This means, just as with Paul, "for wise and holy purposes, best known to himself, [God] hath unloosed my tongue and put his word in my mouth."[93]

Of course, in this section, Stewart makes use of a variety of biblical references to explain the divine mystery of her call, but the section as a whole is run through with Paul.[94] While she makes explicit reference to Deborah, Esther, Mary Magdalene, and the woman of Samaria, her rhetoric ultimately rethinks Paul and argues that he would, indeed, approve of her prophetic ministry: "St. Paul declared that it was shame for a woman to speak in public, yet our great High Priest and Advocate did not condemn the woman for a more notorious offense than this; neither will he condemn this worthless worm. . . . Did St. Paul but know of our wrongs and deprivations, I presume he would make no objection to our pleading in public for our rights."[95] To stand against Maria Stewart at this point means to stand against Paul. It means to stand against the God who called her and called Paul. It means to stand against the God who dwelt with her just as God dwelt with Paul. With the weapon of God's presence, provided in the sign of a particular personalized Pauline scripture, Maria Stewart "set the fiends of the earth and hell at defiance."[96] "Having cast this call as a holy mission from God and feeling thus equipped, Stewart sweeps away any qualms that her sex might disqualify her. . . . She is, she suggests, a woman God has sent to do the job."[97]

CONCLUSION

I conclude now with a few implications we can draw from our analysis of Maria W. Stewart's call narrative and its structure. First, the "truth" presented in Stewart's call narrative does not function primarily as objective information passed from Stewart to the audience. Rather, the spiritual and moral dynamics of her narration come to the fore of her intentions. Her voice, as the *narrator*, participates in the narrative. Thus, the story does not take on the disinterested, objective gaze of academic theology or the self-announced objectivity of the oppressor (male or white). Rather, as a character in the narrative, Stewart's prophetic task lies in embodying or incarnating the *pathos* of God to the people. Indeed, the narrative overflows with so much subjectivity and pathos that it becomes hard to argue against her claims because her "true nature" has become "synonymous with the divine message and one's *pathos* with the divine *pathos*."[98]

Second, we can see a facet of this subjectivity in how narrative time is emphasized over against "real time."[99] Narrative time organizes itself around the themes and concerns of the rhetorical purposes. Stewart's objective does not lie in offering truths of cause and effect. Rather, she organizes her oration around well-known prophetic themes and relies on their order for her chronology.[100] Thus, I discern that the duration and details of the narrative get modified according to how each narrator selects time's relevance to their theme, audience, and rhetorical situation. Historical time remains subjugated to story time; historical happenings, to narrative needs.

Next, the discipline of rhetorical criticism has not always paid attention to the racial or religious components involved in Black women's rhetoric. Future scholarship must take seriously the intersection of gender, race, and religion in Black women's pursuit of liberation *while also* taking seriously the rhetorical situation in which Black women speak. Their intersectional experiences always remain relevant, but sometimes Black women choose to directly attack the racial and gendered patriarchy in their contexts by using tools like the Bible, which white feminists sometimes find oppressive and regressive. However, Black women have found liberation in these texts precisely because they interpret, embody, and read them in liberatory ways, which includes, as demonstrated with Stewart, a keen attentiveness not merely to individual texts but also the structures of texts. Black women find these religious texts liberative precisely because of their complex, advanced, and decidedly liberationist hermeneutic.

Finally, these observations raise significant questions about the secular-sacred, public-private dichotomies we often assume in our discipline. Stewart narrates her story by mixing secular and sacred time, themes, and concerns. She does not divide political and religious commitments. She even challenges masculine-feminine binaries by adopting a prophetic persona generally assumed exclusively by men. Indeed, her speaking presence in public dismantles the public-private binary of the cult of true womanhood. Jacqueline Jones Royster and Gesa E. Kirsch point to our discipline's need to rethink our binaries when they argue that in examining a woman's sermons/speeches, we push "beyond the public-private dichotomy and beyond just calling attention to social networks. Instead, we shift attention more dramatically toward circulations that may have escaped our attention, that we may not have valued."[101]

Maria's Stewart fills her speeches with scripture references because she does not see herself trapped within a binary that reduces her to a political commentator, a civil rights activist, or a protowomanist thinker. Rather, she accepts the mantle of a Black Christian prophet in all its rhetorical, non-dichotomized implications. To sanitize Stewart's voice by forcing her back into modernist binaries means to lose the connections between her speeches and her primary source of strength, political resistance, and worldview. In the use of these various biblical texts, Maria Stewart subverts the racial patriarchy of white America and the gendered patriarchy of Black males. Rather than denigrating her call, these texts align her with the motifs of the Hebrew prophetic-call narratives of the Bible. Stewart's call narrative intertextually links hers with those of Jeremiah and Isaiah. The content of her message reflects that of Ezekiel's. Her ethos and orientation toward suffering surpasses that of James, John, and her male contemporaries. Further, in spite of the Pauline household codes that call for her submission to male authority, Maria W. Stewart narratively embodies Paul's apostolic, prophetic mission. The ultimate form of domestication would be to remove her from these radical claims wherein she imagines and reimagines an egalitarian, sociopolitically liberated Black womanhood. In these ways, Stewart's call narrative stands as subversive and paradigmatic.

CHAPTER 2

The Call Narrative of Richard Allen

THE SACRALIZED SECULAR IN RICHARD ALLEN'S
GOSPEL LABOURS

I used oftimes to pray sitting, standing, or lying; and while my hands were employed to earn my bread, my heart was devoted to my dear Redeemer. Sometimes I would awake from my sleep preaching and praying. I was after this employed in driving of a wagon in time of the continental war, in drawing salt from Rehobar, Sussex county, in Delaware. I had my regular stops and preaching places on the road. I enjoyed many happy seasons in meditation and prayer while in this employment. . . .

They asked me if I would preach for them. I preached for them the next evening. We had a glorious meeting. They invited me to stay till Sabbath day, and preach for them. I agreed to do so, and preached on Sabbath day to a large congregation of different persuasions, and my dear Lord was with me, and I believe there were many souls cut to the heart, and were added to the ministry. They insisted on me to stay longer with them. I stayed and laboured in Radnor several weeks. Many souls were awakened, and cried aloud to the Lord to have mercy upon them. I was frequently called upon by many inquiring what they should do to be saved. I appointed them to prayer and supplication at the throne of grace, and to make use of all manner of prayer, and pointed them to the invitation of our Lord and Saviour Jesus Christ, who has said, "Come unto me, all ye that are weary and heavy laden, and I will give you rest." Glory be to God! and now I know he was a

God at hand and left not afar off. I preached my farewell sermon, and left these dear people. It was a time of visitation from above. Many were the slain of the Lord. Seldom did I ever experience such a time of mourning and lamentation among a people. There were but few coloured people in the neighbourhood—the most of my congregation was white. Some said, this man must be a man of God; I never heard such preaching before. . . .

February, 1786, I came to Philadelphia. Preaching was given out for me at five o'clock in the morning at St. George's Church. I strove to preach as well as I could, but it was a great cross to me; but the Lord was with me. We had a good time, and several souls were awakened, and were earnestly seeking redemption in the blood of Christ. I thought I would stop in Philadelphia a week or two. I preached at different places in the city. My labour was much blessed. I soon saw a large field open in seeking and instructing my African brethren, who had been a long forgotten people and few of them attended public worship. I preached in the commons, in Southwark, Northern Liberties, and wherever I could find an opening. I frequently preached twice a day, at 5 o'clock in the morning and in the evening, and it was not uncommon for me to preach from four to five times a day. I established prayer meetings; I raised a society in 1786 of forty-two members. I saw the necessity of erecting a place of worship for the coloured people. I proposed it to the most respectable people of colour in this city; but here I met with opposition. I had but three coloured brethren that united with me in erecting a place of worship—the Rev. Absalom Jones, William White, and Dorus Ginnings.

—RICHARD ALLEN, *THE LIFE, EXPERIENCE, AND GOSPEL LABOURS OF THE RT. REV. RICHARD ALLEN*[1]

From the beginning of Richard Allen's 1830 autobiography, the narrative reads less like a memoir and more like an apologia, an attempt to defend his prophetic message, activity, and the founding of Mother Bethel AME Church. The narrative progresses with a series of sharp contrasts and unanswered questions that remain rather glaring if we expect a straightforward autobiographical narrative. Richard S. Newman highlights these oddities by contrasting them with the literary milieu just after Allen's age. Newman observes that Allen stated at the very outset of his narrative that "slavery is a bitter pill," a lesson he learned early (as a slave separated from his family) and often (Allen was mistakenly grabbed as a runaway slave in the early 1800s). But Allen stopped there, telling readers merely that he would eventually purchase his freedom. What happened to his mother? How did he react when informed that he would be separated from his parents? Did he ever attempt to reconnect lost family members? Allen's reticence on such matters is interesting when one considers that he died just prior to a literary revolution: the advent of the antebellum slave narratives. Befitting a romantic, confessional, highly emotional age, with a more literate reading republic than ever before, these new style autobiographies of the 1840s and 1850[s] revealed slaves' innermost thoughts to a largely white, Northern, middle-class audience hungry for tales of injustice in the South.[2]

Still, as Newman continues, such emotional vulnerability and openness were foreign to Allen's style and personality. Allen may have thought "veiling one's deeper thoughts was critical to black survival."[3]

The realities of his personality and cultural setting may also explain why, in contrast to Maria W. Stewart, Richard Allen's call narrative in *Gospel Labours* seems much more subtle. If Stewart's call narrative appeared paradigmatic and mimetic of biblical precedent, Allen's must be *found* within a document seeking primarily to argue for the necessity of a Black Methodist congregation and a movement that stands outside white ecclesial hegemony. After all, the primary conflict in the narrative, as Joanna Brooks explains, "led [Absalom] Jones and Allen to establish two independent black churches in Philadelphia: Allen founded the Methodist-affiliated Bethel African Church on April 9, 1794, and Jones organized the Protestant Episcopal African Church of Philadelphia on August 12, 1794."[4] Just as Allen avoids emotion or evades questions that later biographers might have wished he had expounded upon, he also does not provide direct insight into his call narrative. He justifies the divine calling upon Bethel Church but seems less interested in his own personal call narrative.

Still, while the structure of Maria W. Stewart's call narrative more closely mimicked the prophets of the Bible, Allen's call narrative is no less shaped by them. Allen's apologetic narration combines deeply thoughtful Protestant exegesis with a liberation theology shaped by the experience of enslavement, the book of Exodus, and the prophet Amos.[5] Again, we see that narration provides an alternative mode of argument that anchors Allen's rhetorical power in the *experience* of Black people in the nineteenth century. This does not mean Allen could not argue in syllogisms. It means instead that in prophetic form, he understands syllogisms and objectivity do not persuade, nor do they—more importantly for prophetic rhetoric—"preserve morally significant events" in the minds of his audience members.[6]

The rhetorical situation of Allen's narration also needs highlighting. Allen planted Mother Bethel African Methodist Episcopal Church in Philadelphia when a burgeoning Black population triggered significant demographic transformations threatening white social status and economic stability. Predictably, white Philadelphians—sometimes themselves European immigrants—resorted to physical violence and psychological intimidation to maintain racial and economic hegemony. Allen's autobiography and call narrative prophetically unveil that the city's racial realities reflected the church's racial segregation. In unveiling white Methodist racial animosity seen in racially segregated worship space, Allen justifies his entrepreneurial work as a church planter and provides us with the *motive* for embracing his call to prophetic ministry.

CLUSTERING AND CLASHING

When Richard Allen uses "gospel labours" in the title of his autobiography, he employs a *perspective by incongruity*, described by Kenneth Burke as "taking a word usually applied to one setting and transferring it to another setting. It is a 'perspective by incongruity,' since he established it by violating the 'properties' of the word in its previous linkages."[7] For Burke, opposing categories—verbal symbols that clash—get thrust together to provide new interpretive possibilities. Thus, in *Gospel Labours*, Allen elevates himself, a formerly enslaved traveling preacher, to the level of the biblical prophets and contrasts his status with the white Methodist churchmen of his day. I trace this contrast through Allen's autobiography by following the breadcrumbs of his use of key contrasting terms, like *gospel* and *labour*.

In this chapter, I use Kenneth Burke's "cluster criticism," a mechanism for determining motive,[8] to analyze Richard Allen's *The Life, Experience, and Gospel Labours of the Rt. Rev. Richard Allen*. I show that various word clusters demonstrate remarkably consistent uses of key terms that valorize Allen's sacralizing of the secular in his *Gospel Labours* while villainizing white Methodist churchmen who maintain a secular-sacred distinction, which inhibits their desire to *work* to spread the gospel. This contrast rhetorically justifies Allen's calling to apostolic and prophetic ministry while also criticizing social and institutional hierarchies.

I begin my analysis by identifying the key terms based on their frequency or intensity. Next, I determine "what goes with what"[9] in Allen's mind. This requires creating clusters from terms associated with key terms and commentating on *how* they relate. Finally, I inspect the explicit and implicit contrasts of those clusters to ascertain Allen's motives, which include (1) justifying his prophetic, apostolic calling, (2) devaluing his opponent's credentials, and (3) rejecting white secular-sacred dichotomies.

IDENTIFICATION OF KEY TERMS

The key terms in Allen's autobiography are *work, labour, serve,* and *preach.* Allen uses them repeatedly throughout his text, particularly in pivotal moments.[10] These terms connect in clusters with terms, images, or metaphors that congregate around them. Sonja K. Foss details the process of cluster criticism as follows:

> This involves a close examination of the rhetoric to identify each place in which each key term appears. The terms that cluster around each key term in each context in which it appears are noted. Terms may cluster around the key terms in various ways. They simply may appear in close proximity to the term, or a conjunction such as *and* may connect the term to the key term. The rhetor may also suggest a cause-and-effect relationship between the key term and another term, suggesting that the one depends on the other or that one is the cause of the other.[11]

HOW IS *WORK* ASSOCIATED WITH ITS CLUSTER?

Throughout Allen's autobiography, he catalogs various places he found employment. *Work* occurs nine times,[12] seven of which refer to manual labor (see table 1). The ninth reference, regarding the building of a church according to the will of God,[13] mixes manual labor and divine desire in a way that highlights several other uses of the term. While Allen exclusively uses *work* to refer to manual labor, he never distinguishes it from spiritual or religious matters. He works long hours, even skipping church services, so his "unconverted" enslaver will not think religion has made his slaves "worse servants."[14] He further laments his endless toil and the prospect of being sold should his enslaver, Stokely Sturgis, die.[15] This leads him to *work* to purchase his freedom.[16] The economic details of this purchase highlight not merely Allen's work ethic but also his affiliation with Methodist virtues. When Allen accumulated sufficient funds to pay Sturgis for his

Table 1. The key term *work* and its verbal cluster

Term	Charting the cluster	Deeper cluster
	Religion	Does not make servants worse workers
		(Moral) good
		Made better slaves (honesty/industry)
	Freedom	From ceaseless work
	Hard	Versus the ease of his work on his enslaver's plantation
		Hard work led to pain and prayer
	Served my Lord	With manual labour
Work		Head versus heart
	My hands administered to my needs	Received nothing from the (Methodist) connection
		Stopped traveling and went to work
		So no one could say he had violated Methodist institutional rules or committed a chargeable offense
		Industry
		Thank God
	(Building) the house of the Lord	The Lord was with us
		We believed
		(God's) will

freedom, he also offered his debt-ridden owner a significant financial gift, which "testified to Allen's regard for his master and to his adoption of the Methodist disdain for all things that money could buy."[17] As demonstrated in the remainder of this chapter, such disdain for monetary means serves to contrast Allen, a true Methodist, with the white Methodist preachers who demand pay, sometimes inordinate pay, for their services. In Allen's labor, however, he never "forgot to serve my dear Lord,"[18] and he details his prayer life while at *work*. While his hands labored away, his heart remained devoted to his Redeemer.[19]

He also uses *work* to highlight his work ethic. He repeatedly says he never used preaching as a means of making money. When he ran out of clothing, he ceased preaching and began working. In this way, "my hands administered to my necessities."[20]

In these ways, Allen mimics the prophetic-call narrative of the biblical prophet Amos and the apostolic spirit of the apostle Paul. Concerning Amos, the prophet tells us of his absorption in manual labor—shepherding and grooming trees—when God's presence overtook him and called him to his prophetic task.[21] In narrating his story with Amostic parallels, Allen demonstrates the overlap between labor and prophecy. He labors to prophesy; prophesying is labor. He has a call to do both.

The emphasis on manual labor also parallels the apostle Paul in the New Testament. Accused by some in the Corinthian church of making a living, like the Sophists, by using his proclamation of the gospel to become wealthy, Paul responds that he has continued to do manual labor precisely so no one can accuse him of selling his rhetorical talents. In this case, Allen's autobiographical sketch emphasizing his own labor demonstrates that he has never taken advantage of his own rhetorical skill or prophetic gifts for self-benefit. Instead, even after the eventual splintering of his church, he continues to rely on his own labor. No one can accuse Allen of prophesying to make money or achieve acclaim.

HOW IS *LABOUR* ASSOCIATED WITH ITS CLUSTER?

The second term, *labour*, occurs nine times (see table 2). Four refer explicitly to religious labor. The other five initially appear ambiguous because they could reference manual or religious labor. However, of note, not least because *labour* occurs in the autobiography's title, eight of the nine uses of *labour* occur in the same paragraph.[22]

Four times Allen uses the term unambiguously to refer to *gospel* labor or the "awakening" of souls. However, two of the more ambiguous uses are connected to words that suggest that even if the work equates to manual labor, Allen still sees God's presence and favor in that work. The unambiguously religious uses of *labour* surround the ambiguous uses, communicating that Allen sees his primary labor in each community as preaching the gospel.

Table 2. The key term *labour* and its verbal cluster

Term	Charting the cluster
	Gospel
	Preach(ed) (3x)
	Glory
	Faith
	Blessed (3x)
	Served the Lord
Labour	The Lord was with . . . (3x)
	Souls (3x)
	Employed (cutting wood)
	Affliction of body (rheumatism, foot pain) (2x)
	Kindly received
	Added to the ministry
	Large field open for instructing African brethren

Note: Dashed arrow indicates the shift to formal usage.

Manual labor serves the religious end. To use Burke's phrasing, Allen "converts"[23] manual labor upward and makes "secular" labor sacred.

Further, the ambiguous samples not only are surrounded by religious terminology but also contain intertextual biblical references. In one, Allen tells of a family who showed him the ancient Christian virtue of hospitality even though he was physically ill.[24] Such hospitality and caring for the traveling minister intertextually reference Paul's experience with the Galatian church.[25] Like Allen's *Gospel Labours*, Galatians contains a lengthy discussion of Paul's travelogue as he preached throughout the Roman Empire.[26] Moreover, Galatians contains a personal narrative designed, at least in part, to defend Paul's apostolic, prophetic calling. Through this intertextual use of Pauline imagery, Allen identifies himself as an heir or embodiment of the apostle Paul.

Further, Allen's sore feet intertextually reference Romans 10:15, where Paul blesses the feet of those who are sent to preach the gospel.[27] Again, if the exigence for which Allen writes his autobiography is a challenge to his apostolic or prophetic ministry, discussing his sore feet and those who blessed his feet with healing balms would resonate with biblically informed audiences who understand its referent to preachers and prophets of the gospel. Indeed, far more than a reference to Romans 10:15, the man and his wife washing Allen's feet reminds readers of Jesus washing his disciple's feet.[28] The scene not only shows Allen's affection for this couple (placing them in the position of Jesus) but also verifies his claims to apostolic and prophetic authority as one who has received foot washing from Jesus. Allen identifies himself as the heir or embodiment of Paul and the twelve disciples.

In the end, Allen's use of *labour* clusters mostly in one paragraph that is saturated with religious language and intertextually rich. Allen intertwines the labors. *To labor* is to do the Lord's work, whether that work entails preaching or performing manual labor. When referenced at all, manual labor affords him the opportunity to preach.

HOW IS *SERVE* ASSOCIATED WITH ITS CLUSTER?

Allen uses forms of *serve* (serve, service, servant) ten times in *Gospel Labours* (see table 3). Four times they form the phrase "Serve the Lord."[29] Five refer to the vocational service of white preachers who sought inordinate pay. Of these, he never says their service was "for the Lord" even though they were doing church work. None refer to manual labor.

I also discern formal and informal uses of these terms. The informal refers to acts of menial service directed toward or performed by fellow Christians. These include acts of hospitality, healing, or piety. The formal uses refer to the vocation of pastoring a church. He uses the formal exclusively for the white preachers he criticizes.

Table 3. The key term *serve* and its verbal cluster

Term	Charting the cluster	Deeper	Deeper still
	My dear Lord	Hard work	Slavery
	Prayer	My Redeemer	Make my living
	Preaching (7x)		Employed (brickyard, cutting wood, driving wagon)
	My dear Lord (was with me)		
	Blessed		
	Glory to God		
	Family	Trust	
	Labour		
Serve	Loved the Lord (2x)		
	Happy		
	Pious woman	Children are strangers to Christian religion	Preached
	Other ministers: inadequate pay to serve church (2x)		
	Will pay preacher		
	No pastor allowed to serve us	*Pastors expelled if they serve us*	
	Left to ourselves		
	Could not preach		

Note: Dashed arrows and italics indicate the shift to formal usage.

HOW IS *PREACH* ASSOCIATED WITH ITS CLUSTER?

The terms *preach, preacher, preached,* and *preaching* comprise the single most prevalent word family in Allen's autobiography with sixty uses and thus likely comprise the "ultimate term" in the text (see table 4). The uses are overwhelmingly positive except the explicitly negative uses *exclusively* used in reference to the white Methodist ministers in Philadelphia and Baltimore. In all, Allen sees simple Methodist "spiritual" and "extempore"[30] preaching as the source of Methodism's success among people of color. It also converts his enslaver early in the autobiography and persuades him to release enslaved Africans. Preaching "awakens" hundreds of souls throughout the narrative, and Allen hints at no resistance to his own preaching until he encounters white Methodist preachers.[31] He also associates preaching with acts of piety and worship at least six times and laments the loss of such disciplines among the Methodists of his day.

Table 4. The key term *preach* and its verbal cluster

Term	Charting the Cluster	Deeper Cluster
	The gospel	Lord, Savior Jesus (2x), saved
	Acts of piety/worship (6x)	
	Religion made better slaves	Honesty/industry
	Methodist (13x)	First to preach to Black people, skeptical/willing to preach at master's house, simple preaching, abandon discipline
	Master converted	Gave up slave owning
	Woke from sleep preaching/praying	
	Preached while traveling for work (9x)	Happy seasons, meditation, prayer

	Met acquaintances through (5x)	Hospitality, apostle, trustworthy family, souls added to the labour, blessed, great faith
	Lord with me/them (7x)	Blessed labours, glory to God (2x), souls for hire, laboured for the Lord (2x)
	Glorious meeting	
	Souls awakened	Cried to the Lord, seeking redemption, white and coloured
Preach/preacher/ preaching/preached	Must be a man of God	
	English (preachers)	Ministers / holy orders
	St. Georges Church	
	Large field opened to preach to Black people	
	Met opposition (4x)	For building church for coloured people (2x), blotted out opposition names (3x), used insulting language
	White elder would not preach	Persecuted us
	Tyrants	Especially to Black people, rejected by the Methodist society dominated by whites
	Divided money gained from preaching with white preachers	

Term	Charting the Cluster	Deeper Cluster
	1793, appointed to preach in Philadelphia	Only Black preacher in Philadelphia, rejected appointment because Methodist
	White preachers want higher pay than church can afford (13x)	Limited times they would preach because of this pay
	White minister forcing way into the pulpit	Packed around pulpit and kept him from getting in it
	Similar acts by white preachers in Baltimore	

Seven times Allen uses the phrase "The Lord was with me/them" in the context of preaching. The term has intertextual significance with the Bible. Prophetic figures in the Bible often struggle with God's presence when they face opposition. Due to this, they need constant reassurance of divine presence.[32] At other times, the Bible says, "the Lord was with" a prophetic figure, making their prophecies come true and giving them status among the faith community.[33] Allen's sevenfold repetition of this phrase does not merely reflect a habit of the tongue; it identifies him with the biblical prophets.

The negative uses of the term universally refer to the white preachers who use the craft to make money. Allen remains uninterested in whether they can make a living preaching because he has detailed decades of *work* that afforded him the opportunity to preach. He exhibits no sympathy for white preachers who refuse to do manual labor so they can preach but only want to make their living by preaching.

Both by displaying his willingness to *work* to preach and by displaying the white preachers' unwillingness to work, Allen, again, calls upon the apostle Paul. Acts 18:3 describes Paul's travels to Corinth, where he stayed for a season with a couple and did manual labor (tent making) with them. Acts 18:4, then, connects Paul's manual labor with the work of preaching the gospel as he used his time working in Corinth to visit local synagogues and evangelize.[34] Allen's subtle use of the Pauline tent-making theme further contrasts him and the white Methodists. Despite their denominational credentials, it justifies his apostolic, prophetic calling and calls theirs into question.

VIEW OF KEY TERMS REVEALED IN THEIR OPPOSITES

The next step in cluster criticism involves analyzing the implicit and explicit *contrasts* of Allen's key terms. I begin by charting their opposites. From there, I offer thoughts on how the clusters work within Allen's autobiography.

Through this analysis of opposites, we see Allen's derisive critique of his opponents. By "converting" manual labor upward and making it sacred, Allen rhetorically prepares his readers for moral judgment long before he introduces the opponents in the climax of his text. In all four opposites sets, the negative involves a lack of divine activity or presence (see table 5). His opposites are implicit in the first three key terms, and he makes them explicit with the white Methodist preachers. Allen laments their lack of attention to Methodist disciplines, disinterest in piety, refusal to *serve* Black churches, and tyranny.[35] By contrasting their *service* with his *labor*, he suggests they do not experience the divine presence. Due to this lack, they have no passion for converting the "African brethren," something for which Methodists have had a reputation.[36] He attributes these failures to such Methodists "becoming somebody" instead of remaining on the margins, seeking status instead of associating with nobodies.[37] Dickerson coincides this lament with a shift in class demographics in eighteenth- and nineteenth-century Methodists. "The Wesleyan movement that initially drew Allen's loyalty became an increasingly unfamiliar religious body. The fervor with which the gospel was advanced, openness to the poor and to blacks, and staunch abolitionism all started to wane."[38] Such preachers can never be recognized as "men of God"[39] or embody the prophetic and scriptural narratives as Allen does. Despite their credentials, he rhetorically reduces them to tyrants and bullies, men who merely *preach* but are unwilling to *work* for it.

Table 5. Oppositional binaries related to the key terms

View of *work* revealed in cluster analysis	Opposite[1]
Hard working (Christian) servants/slaves	A religion that creates lazy servants
Honesty	*Falsity*
Industry	*Lack of work ethic*
Serve the Lord	*Unconverted/self-interested*

View of *work* revealed in cluster analysis	Opposite[1]
My hands were employed to earn my bread, my heart was devoted to my dear Redeemer	*Work without devotion to God*
Worked to meet needs	Burden on the connection
View of *labour* revealed in cluster analysis	Opposite
Blessing	*Nonblessed* (he never says "cursed")
Preaching	Refusal to preach without inordinate pay
Faith	*Unfaithful*
Serve the Lord	*Unfaithfulness*
Awakened souls	*Cannot awaken souls*
Welcomed me	Opposed me
Added to the ministry	*Fruitless*
I soon saw a large field open in seeking and instructing my African brethren, who had been long forgotten	*No concern to evangelize*
View of *serve* revealed in cluster analysis	Opposite
Serve	"Serve" only when paid
Serve the Lord	*Self-interested*
Prayer	*Prayerlessness*
The Lord was with me/us	Removed Black members from the congregation and Methodist society
Shared with white ministers	Require pay to preach
Laboured for the Lord	Do not want to preach at poor Black churches

View of *preach* revealed in cluster analysis	Opposite
Preacher	Refusal to do manual labour
Souls awakened	*Will not see souls awakened*
Recognized as a "man of God"	*Will not be recognized as "a man of God"*
Piety and spiritual discipline	Disregards piety and discipline
The Lord was with me/them	*Those who do not experience the Lord's presence*
Those who serve the church (informally)	Tyrants, refuse to work to preach, bullies

1. The *implied* contrasts are italicized to differentiate them from the explicit rhetorical contrasts.

THOUGHTS ON MOTIVES

Foss says naming motives involves answering the question, "Given that these terms have special meanings for this rhetor, what was the motive for producing this particular rhetoric in this specific way likely to have been?"[40] Burke argues for four fundamental motives in human communication: guilt, redemption, hierarchy, and victimage.[41] While Allen tells his story with antagonists, he does not frame the story in terms of victimage. He also expresses no guilt and therefore no need for redemption. His primary motive seems to be hierarchical. *Gospel Labours* elevates him spiritually and denominationally above the white Methodist preachers in Philadelphia. His rhetoric functions to "convert upward" notions of *labor, work,* and *service* so that they are seen on the same sacred plane as *preaching.* I end this chapter by discussing various ways Allen's upward-converting rhetoric dismantles hierarchies and breaks down binaries that propped up white religious presumptions.

APOSTLE AND PROPHET

Through explicitly identifying himself with the biblical prophets and the apostle Paul, Richard Allen elevates his status beyond merely a formerly enslaved traveling preacher or church planter. He demonstrates through these clusters that from the beginning, his primary concern has been the promulgation of the gospel—no matter the cost. In his bruised feet made beautiful through his preaching travels, his tent making like the apostle Paul, and even in his travelogue, Allen identifies with the biblical narrative in a way that both incarnates its narrative and makes him consubstantial with biblically literate audiences. The motive lies in a favorable hierarchy wherein he contrasts himself with white Methodist preachers who refuse to work and therefore cannot embody the biblical narrative or prophetic discourses. As an ex-slave and traveling preacher, his prophetic and apostolic credentials outweigh his counterparts, thus placing him in a higher spiritual position. He has justified his call to apostolic and prophetic ministry and has delegitimized the *service* of those with all the institutional, formal credentials. The human hierarchy has it wrong, but then again, institutions have rarely appreciated the prophets in their midst.

PROPHETS AND BINARIES

Kenneth Burke highlights the complexity of determining motive when he says that "it will naturally take its place within the framework of our *Weltanschauung* as a whole."[42] Rooted in this, he continues, "We discern situational patterns by means of the particular vocabulary of the cultural group into which we are born. Our minds, as linguistic products, are composed of concepts which select certain relationships as meaningful ... these relationships are not *realities*; they are *interpretations* of reality."[43] Because of these interpretations of reality and motives, we must understand the dominance of our own (post)modern dichotomies, which would not make sense to either the Hebrew prophets or nineteenth-century Black figures. Richard Allen cannot speak in terms of a secular-sacred dichotomy because it remains foreign to his experience as an enslaved person where life is *work* and God speaks in that *work*.

Prophetic rejection of inconvenient or artificial binaries fills the Bible. Allen heavily relies upon the prophetic books of the Bible to reject the false binaries of his opponents. Isaiah's call narrative, for example, brings together "Holy, Holy, Holy"—signifying the transcendence and distance of Yahweh— with "the whole earth is full of his glory"—indicating the immanence and presence of Yahweh.[44] The whole earth (immanence) is full of God's glory (transcendence). With the collapse of the binaries, a whole host of collapses occurs. As Abraham J. Heschel points out:

God and the world are not opposite poles. There is darkness in the world, but there is also this call, "Let there be light!" Nor are body and soul at loggerheads. We are not told to decide between "Either-Or," either God or the world, either this world or the world to come. We are told to accept Either and Or, God and the world. It is upon us to strive for a share in the world to come, as well as to let God have a share in this world.[45]

There are no secular-sacred, no body-soul, no this-worldly–next-worldly binaries.

Such nondualistic thinking reveals why, as Newman points out, "Allen was comfortable with secular and sacred texts. He read not only Josephus but also works by contemporary American statesmen, including both Ben Franklin and George Washington."[46] God's presence permeated the secular and sacred histories, politics, and philosophies.

Enlightenment binaries riddled white theology and kept it shackled to its own oppressive categories, but Molefi Kete Asante makes an important point that applies to Allen when he says, "No black man can truly identify with a God who speaks only the language of the white oppressor."[47] The dualistic, binary-laden language of whiteness would have inhibited Allen's ability to critique his opponents. The rejection—or transcendence—of such language provided him prophetic insight that changed American history, even if some scholars still cannot see it. For a prophetic figure heralding the fulfillment of Methodist promises of equality, Allen's "best claims to equal founding status was his attempt to merge faith and racial politics in the young republic."[48]

WHY SO NONDRAMATIC?

Compared to Maria W. Stewart, Nat Turner, and Julia Foote, Richard Allen's call narrative appears, to use William H. Myers's terminology, noncataclysmic.[49] In such narratives, the prophet does not experience a complete reorientation during their calling. Instead, the calling occurs as a natural overflow at the intersection of their theology, politics, and life. Christopher Z. Hobson comments on a similar experience with other figures in the African American prophetic tradition: "Most of my subjects, however, do not claim to act by commandment. One reason may be that those with formal study in divinity generally accepted the tradition that God's direct authorization of prophecy had ceased after the canonical prophets. Additionally, Methodists and Baptists recognized speech inspired by the Holy Spirit—but not directly commanded by God—as more authoritative than ordinary pastoral speech."[50] Whether or not Allen views direct communication with God as having ceased remains irrelevant. Hobson's point lies in the fact that receiving a calling to prophecy need not require a cataclysmic visionary event.

However, something beyond educational bias may lay behind Allen's noncataclysmic calling. He may have no need to breakdown a hierarchy that might exclude him. Specifically, Allen holds the most social privilege of our four figures. As a *freeman*, he has more social privilege than Nat Turner. He has more social privilege than either Foote or Stewart as a *man*. Further, the fact that he has enough social clout among the Black community in Philadelphia to start a new church suggests that a dramatic visionary tale was not needed to convince anyone of his ethos or social belonging.

THE SACRALIZED SECULAR IN ALLEN'S *GOSPEL LABOURS*

When Richard Allen calls his autobiography *Gospel Labours*, he deliberately cultivates the use of contradictory concepts, particularly among Protestants who see the gospel as "grace not works." Allen employs a rhetorical perspective by incongruity whereby spiritual pieties (the gospel) are conjoined to material pieties[51] (labor) in a way that provides a new orientation toward the task of preaching. Allen never separates the spiritual and material but continually presses them together in *abab* structure through his narrative. "Instead of looking for a Hegelian synthesis that would follow thesis and antithesis, he would have us realize that the real course of events is necessarily, at all times, unified."[52] Allen's problem with the white Methodist preachers lies precisely in their desire to do the spiritual work of preaching without the material work of manual labor. Allen sees gospel and labors, together, as the means by which his hands and his heart are conjoined. His rhetoric "converts upward" the Black, traveling, tent-making prophet and converts downward the white Methodist preachers who separate the secular and sacred. Instead of working within a secular-sacred dichotomy, Allen cannot separate the two. Instead, he finds the *gospel* solely in the context of *labors* and understands *labor* as the only means for preaching the *gospel*.

This conflation of secular and sacred in *Gospel Labours* forms a perspective by incongruity that aligns Allen with the larger Black church liberationist theology and African American prophetic tradition. Dianna Watkins-Dickerson calls prophetic utterance "the moment in which the sacred and the secular, much like blues and gospel, converge upon one another."[53] Asante explains, "The Afrocentric writer knows that oppositional dichotomies do not exist. . . . The interaction of my physical and metaphysical world leads to my behavior at the moment and this interaction cannot be reduced to separate units,"[54] such as body and mind, material and spiritual, secular and sacred, or private and public. These categories have been read onto African American rhetoric.[55] Part of Allen's motive in his autobiography lies precisely in demonstrating the superiority of the *preacher*, prophet, or apostle who leaves these elements in a holistic harmony rather than, as the white Methodist preachers do, assuming a secular-sacred divide that allows one to merely *preach* without *working*, *serving*, or *doing gospel labor*.

CHAPTER 3

The Call Narrative of Julia Foote

SELF-LOVE AND SUBVERSIVE SANCTIFICATION

For months I had been moved upon to exhort and pray with the people, and my visits from house to house; and in meetings my whole soul seemed drawn out for the salvation of souls. The love of Christ in me was not limited. Some of my mistaken friends said I was too forward, but a desire to work for the Master, and to promote the glory of his kingdom in the salvation of souls, was food to my poor soul.

When called of God, on a particular occasion, to a definite work, I said, "No, Lord, not me." Day by day I was more impressed that God would have me work in his vineyard. I thought it could not be that I was called to preach—I, so weak and ignorant. Still I knew all things were possible with God, even to confounding the wise by the foolish things of this earth. Yet in me there was a shrinking.

I took all my doubts and fears to the Lord and prayer, when, what seemed to be an angel made his appearance. In his hand there was a scroll, on which were these words: "Thee have I chosen to preach my Gospel without delay." The moment my eye saw it, it appeared to be printed on my heart. The angel was gone in an instant, and I, in agony, cried out, "Lord, I cannot do it!" It was eleven o'clock in the morning, yet everything grew dark as night. The darkness was so great that I feared to stir. . . .

One night, as I lay weeping and beseeching the dear Lord to remove this burden from me, there appeared the same angel that came to me before, and on his breast were these words: "You are lost unless you obey God's righteous commands." I saw the writing, and that was enough. I covered my head and awoke my husband, who had returned a few days before. He asked me why I trembled so much, but I had not power to answer him. I remained in that condition until morning, when I tried to arise and go about my usual duties, but was too ill. Then my husband called a physician, who prescribed medicine, but it did me no good.

I had always been opposed to the preaching of women, and had spoken against it, though, I acknowledge, without foundation. This rose before me like a mountain, and when I thought of the difficulties they had to encounter, both from professors and non-professors, I shrink back and cried, "Lord, I cannot go!"

—JULIA FOOTE, *A BRAND PLUCKED FROM THE FIRE: AN AUTOBIOGRAPHICAL SKETCH*[1]

For most of her faith journey, Julia Foote forbade female preaching. Like many of her contemporaries, she assumed women should serve "the church in some type of domestic position as members of the congregation, benevolent aid organizers, or Sunday school teachers."[2] She submitted to male spiritual and familial authority and "posed no real threat to the power structure maintained by preachers, deacons, and other male leaders."[3]

By the end of her life, however, having experienced the socially subversive bush meetings of the Second Great Awakening, years of denominational infighting, and even exile from her church, Foote had become the first female deaconess and full elder in the AME Zion denomination. She even participated in revivals in Canada, across the northeastern United States, and deep into the Midwest, at one juncture preaching to a crowd of several thousand. These and other tales of her prophetic fire and protofeminist rhetoric appear in her autobiography, *A Brand Plucked from the Fire*, wherein she prophetically applied the Methodist doctrine of entire sanctification to racial and gendered discrimination and the structural, legal, and financial hinderances to Black flourishing in America.

The movement in her narrative from rejecting her call to preach to becoming a revivalist started when she began having visionary experiences wherein God called her to preach through an angelic intermediary. In a period of liminality, she wrestled with reticence and repeatedly responded to God, "No, Lord, not me."[4] In arguing with God, she appealed to her impotence and ignorance, wavering back and forth between knowing "all things are possible with God" and a "shrinking" feeling of dread.[5] When taking these doubts and fears before God in prayer, she experienced successive "heavenly visitations," which grew increasingly colorful and climaxed with an apocalyptic trip to heaven wherein the Holy Trinity directly revealed divine will to her, connected her gospel preaching to the Hebrew prophet Joel,[6] and compelled her to surrender to the call to preach. Foote's surrender, however, proved the easiest part of her prophetic journey because outside her heavenly visions—indeed, in the church—patriarchy and white supremacy persisted.

This chapter utilizes the insights of womanism to examine Julia Foote's call narrative from her autobiography, *A Brand Plucked from the Fire*. A fascinating amalgamation of slave autobiography and spiritual autobiography, Foote's narrative employs a protowomanist hermeneutic of redemptive self-love as a means of authenticating her prophetic and apostolic calling. Further, Foote's call narrative elucidates a rhetorical theology of redemptive self-love that refutes the reticence of "professors and non-professors,"[7] her spouse,[8] her mother,[9] her pastor,[10] white people in general, her audience, her denomination, and, most importantly, herself. Beginning with a discussion of womanism and redemptive self-love as a theoretical framework for reading Foote's rhetoric, I then discuss redemptive self-love within the context of Foote's *conscious* choice of genre and the conscious choices involved in crafting a call narrative that counters the hegemonies of whiteness and patriarchy. Finally, I discuss facets of her call narrative that orient the reader around the notions of redemptive self-love, including her emphasis on entire sanctification, her application of apocalyptic imagery, her employment of Edenic and Eve-related imagery, and, finally, her intimate cleansing from Christ.

In Foote's description of her call narrative, we get a unique insight into prophecy's emphasis on pathos. Abraham J. Heschel highlights pathos as the prime rhetorical tool of the prophet, particularly as pathos reflects the passions of God:

> An analysis of prophetic utterances shows us that the fundamental experience of the prophet is a fellowship with the feelings of God, *a sympathy with divine pathos,* a communion with the divine consciousness which comes about through the prophet's reflection of, or participation in, the divine pathos. The typical prophetic state of mind is one of being taken up into the heart of the divine pathos. . . . The emotional experience of the prophet becomes the focal point for the prophet's understanding of God. He lives not only his personal life, but also the life of God.[11]

Thus, in the pathos-filled narrativization of her prophetic call, Julia Foote, like many other female prophets before and after her, *embodies* the prophetic prediction of Joel 3:1–2, which promises the Holy Spirit's empowerment of *all* flesh, including women's, to prophecy with the pathos of God. Women like Foote have found their voice authorized by Joel's words when expanded such that "all people, without regard to gender, age, or social standing, will function as prophets."[12]

WOMANISM AS THE BEST FOOTE FORWARD

Until recently, few scholars in communication and specifically rhetoric have paid attention to womanism or its ancestry. Womanism's practitioners have concentrated on activism rather than academics, survival rather than systemization. Kimberly P. Johnson rightly observes, "More people have employed womanism than have described it."[13] However, this inattention has shifted with more womanists writing scholastically and more scholars reading womanist works. This amalgamation has inaugurated a fresh academic arena ablaze with opportunities to reassess familiar voices, excavate forgotten ones, and distinguish Black women's experiences from Black men and white women. For example, whereas "feminist scholars have reasoned that women's language, acts, and deeds of liberation tended to express themselves quite differently than those of men,"[14] womanists have added that Black women's language, acts, and deeds of liberation tend to express themselves quite differently than those of white women. Womanism allows us to reengage Black women's voices and asks how their rhetoric, agenda, activism, and assumptions all differ from those of the white feminists.

Through this reengagement, we realize one remarkable difference between feminism and womanism lies in the degree of openness to Christianity. Feminism has, with warrant, largely left the church and considered the Bible as an apparatus of androcentric autocracy. Womanists, however, while still acknowledging the patriarchal presumptions in the Black church and white interpretations of the Bible, read themselves into the biblical narrative, see themselves as actors who embody the ongoing, open-ended narrative, and employ their incarnation of the biblical narrative to subvert patriarchy and white supremacy. Johnson asks with feminists and womanists alike, "What can be said when the churches where we worship are intoxicated with patriarchal religious traditions and rhetoric? How can we turn to the church for affirmation, guidance, and strength if the messages that we hear from the pulpit only seem to liberate and affirm the humanity of our male counterparts?

Where do we go to get the information on what strategies to use?"[15] Whereas feminists may reply to Johnson's queries by dismissing the church as a pillar of patriarchy, Johnson answers with an appeal to the experiences of Black female preachers of the gospel who intentionally interpret the Bible with an eye toward the experiences of Black women's liberation. Instead of merely having the Bible laid over them and theology taught to them, womanist rhetoric centralizes Black women's subjectivity in producing discourses of knowledge and power, and their bodies become "conduits of the divine."[16]

Contemporary womanists did not, however, invent a biblical herme-neutic of liberation or emancipatory methods of knowledge production. They inherited these from protowomanists, like Julia Foote: "[The] bibli-cal hermeneutic applied by early black women's autobiographers to their social situation is not unlike the womanist hermeneutic valorized by latter twentieth-century and twenty-first-century womanist biblical scholars such as Renita Weems, who contends that 'womanist biblical hermeneutical reflections do not begin with the Bible' but with 'African American women's will to survive and thrive as human beings.'"[17] To survive and thrive as human beings, Black women historically had to learn to love themselves as *Black* and as *women*. Womanist academics adopted the language of "redemptive self-love" to articulate their effort to love themselves in oppo-sition to the antagonisms of androcentrism and whiteness. Indeed, more than themselves, in a rejection of white individualism (another contrast with white feminism), womanist activists and rhetoricians have focused on "principles of justice for the entire community."[18] In the classic words of Alice Walker, a womanist commits to the "survival and wholeness of entire people, male and female. . . . Womanist is to feminist as purple is to lavender."[19] Thus, redemptive self-love not only applies to Black women but also typifies their prophetic proclamation to all people, whether white or Black, male or female.

Womanism's openness to religious experience is anticipated in the tradi-tions of nineteenth-century Black women's spiritual autobiographers. Julia Foote's *A Brand Plucked from the Fire* is not unique in the employment of religious experience as a means of empowering women to "appropriate their own moral agency to move, to challenge, and to reinterpret reality differently than the prevailing social norms and power structures dictated."[20] In wom-anist terms, religious experiences helped women like Foote love themselves and find their voices in a "white man's" world. As with nineteenth-century protowomanist preaching, so too with contemporary womanist preaching: redemptive self-love expanding outward to the entire community drives the womanist's rhetorical theology. What Johnson says about contemporary

womanist homiletics equally applies to the rhetoric of nineteenth-century
Black women's spiritual autobiographies:

> Redemptive self-love sermons seek to redeem a woman by remov-
> ing the socially perceived shame of a woman away from her actions.
> The preacher must offer a perspectival corrective that re-images the
> woman from being a villain to being a heroine by identifying the
> integrity and morals by which the woman lives to lift the shame,
> dishonor, disgrace, and condemnation that society has placed upon
> the woman. These sermons also require the preacher to encourage
> women (both in the text and in the audience) to match their human
> agency and moral agency with a rhetorical agency. Redemptive self-
> love reflects the ability to unashamedly love self and stand up for self
> regardless of what anyone else thinks.[21]

This womanist value and voyage toward redemptive self-love drive even
the rhetorical choices of protowomanists like Julia Foote. She asserted her
humanity by employing first-person narration and a creative interpretation
of biblical texts.

Feminist theologian Elisabeth Schussler Fiorenza highlights five aspects
of feminist biblical criticism and theological method: (1) hermeneutic of
suspicion, (2) hermeneutic of remembrance, (3) hermeneutic of imagination, (4) hermeneutic of evaluation and proclamation, and (5) hermeneutic
of resistance.[22] Womanism adds to Fiorenza's list (6) radical subjectivity,
(7) traditional communalism, (8) redemptive self-love, and (9) critical
engagement.[23] By placing themselves as subjects within the biblical narrative, they ground their interpretive authority within the communal assessment of other Black women who mutually attempt to build what Martin
Luther King Jr. called "the Beloved Community."[24] The Beloved Community
serves as a realized (i.e., present) eschatological (i.e., end-times) community wherein the Christian prophetic vision of a future egalitarian, just
society comes to fruition in the present. It is a communal reality that refuses
this-worldly and next-worldly binaries. As Annette D. Madlock explains,
the Beloved Community is

> an inclusive space where all people share in the wealth of the earth,
> and where poverty, hunger, homelessness, and other forms of social
> injustice are not tolerated. Peaceful conflict resolution prevails where
> love and trust triumph over fear and hatred, and all God's children
> rejoice in peace and justice. . . . A womanist ethos, logos, and pathos

rejects oppression and is committed to social justice and inclusivity for all of humanity; this is the set of values that goes beyond theology.[25]

The prophetic nature of this community gets highlighted further by Katie Geneva Cannon. She writes that in the womanist community, "Black women serve as contemporary prophets, calling other women forth so that they can break away from the oppressive ideologies and belief systems that presume to define their reality."[26]

Thus, womanist theology and rhetoric situate Black women's subjectivity at the center of the biblical narrative and its intersection with contemporary life in the biblical fight against oppression and empire. Centering Black women's experiences requires a critique of white feminism and Black (including the Black church's) patriarchy.[27] It requires a dismantling of the binaries of patriarchy in all its forms that keep Black women from attaining their full personhood through intersectional sites of oppression.[28]

Rhetorical critics have largely overlooked the contribution of womanists and protowomanists,[29] which seems particularly problematic given the possibilities they offer for further dismantling the hold patriarchy still has in our discipline. In this chapter, I offer a glimpse into the beauty of womanist rhetorical, theological, and ideological contributions by demonstrating that Julia Foote, a protowomanist, "engaged in the process of knowledge production that [was] most necessary for [her] own flourishing rather than being exploited for the enlightenment and entertainment of white psyches and male egos."[30]

REDEMPTIVE SELF-LOVE AND RHETORICAL CHOICES

GENRE

Discourse analysts define genre as "a recognizable communicative event characterized by a set of communicative purposes identified and mutually understood by members of the community in which it occurs."[31] Because a genre has a recognized structure, includes discursive intentions, *is* a social action, and happens within a community that understands those intentions, the rhetor never passively chooses a genre. Further, through genre, rhetors gather the discourse community into a common set of goals, self-articulations, ambitions, and actions. By mastering genre, rhetors reinforce belonging and assert their rightful place in the discourse community. "We produce and use genres not just in order to get things done but also to show ourselves to be members of particular groups and to demonstrate that we are qualified to participate in particular activities."[32]

So when Julia Foote selects spiritual autobiography as the genre to tell her story, she asserts her membership in a community historically off-limits to her. She and her audience both know spiritual autobiography "is more representative of the 'straight white Christian man of property' and privilege who has been valorized as the unmarked 'universal' subject."[33] By choosing a genre associated with the "universal" white male subject, Julia Foote establishes herself, a Black woman, as a member and actor[34] within the universal human community, as a prophet to the universal human community to whom God has called her. Through this choice of genre, she places herself, her calling, her actions, and her religious experience on equal footing with white male Christian preachers of privilege. She takes a genre that valorizes white men and applies it to a Black woman. She accomplishes the genre's goals not through glamourizing the usual subjects but by sanctifying the unexpected subjects. Before her audience reads a word, they know her genre choice carries socially subversive significance: Black women, no less than white men, can love themselves enough to tell their own stories; no less than white men, Black women have claims to human agency and subjectivity.

William L. Andrews cites two other relevancies of autobiography to Black women's self-narration: (1) a demonstration of the author's humanity and (2) the establishment of the narrator as truth teller.[35] Cannon combines these when she says, "The Black women's literary tradition delineates the many ways that ordinary Black women have fashioned value patterns and ethical procedures in their own terms, as well as mastering, transcending, radicalizing and sometimes destroying pervasive, negative orientations imposed by the mores of larger society."[36] However, this rewriting of pervasive negative orientations involves a communal process, not merely individual resistance. Collectively, Black women created a *Black counterpublic* in which they found mutual support and affirmation.[37] Part of this counterpublic entails the production of literary materials that center Black women's subjectivity, humanity, and truth over against the objectivity, dehumanization, and lies of white male supremacy: "Counterpublics foster political and cultural activities that allow working-class and other disfranchised persons to reclaim a measure of subjectivity despite being positioned as the instruments, objects, or properties of the middle class. The counterpublic . . . stages a social and discursive challenge to the power of the white male property owners who make up civil society."[38] The distinctiveness of a Black woman's self-narration is coupled with the complexity of the historical record and personal recollection, which change with time and telling. This rings true especially in Black autobiographies because, as John Ernest argues, certain literary structures become standardized in the attempts to assert Black humanity and truth telling. Thus, "the vision of history that black autobiography could offer was, accordingly, predetermined."[39] Thus, Foote's "autobiographical sketch of her call fits squarely in the long history of the African American call narrative tradition, which dates back to the period of African enslavement in America."[40]

NARRATIVE SHAPE

Scholars have long noted the centrality of religious storytelling and its function as self-affirmation in the African American rhetorical tradition. However, as noted throughout this book, minimal academic attention has accented African American call narratives and the rhetorical devices employed therein.[41] Despite this inattention, these narratives matter—not only for their vivid imagery and insight into nineteenth-century Black religion but also because we gain insight into how figures like Julia Foote saw themselves through their rhetorical theology. "To critically examine the first-person narratives of some African American women as they relate the stories surrounding their calls to ministry, privileging the centrality of the women's language, is to know how these women see the world and to use a womanist consciousness to interrogate voice, community, and identity."[42]

Words create worlds, and the worlds created in these call narratives depict a dynamic deity who continues to narrate redemption beyond the biblical canon. Despite the near Deism of white Christianity, whose doctrines declared that God had spoken a final word in the Bible and did not directly communicate in the present, Julia Foote held that God currently calls and declares definitive words directly to individuals "when called of God, on a particular occasion, to a definite work."[43] "Called" requires a response. "Particular occasion" places Foote's calling within a specific earthly timeframe, not a general spiritual feeling or a mystical otherworldly experience. "To a definitive work" stipulates the specifics of the labor she should undertake. Nothing about this experience conveys subjective abstractions, merely mysticism, or even emotivism. Foote's rhetorical theology asserts that God still acts definitively and speaks specifics to the world through the unexpected, unwanted perspective of a reticent Black woman. Thomas Hoyt Jr. provocatively says, "By telling a story, one could create or destroy a world view,"[44] and Julia Foote articulates her story in a way that destroys the worldview of Christianized Deism, ecclesial androcentrism, and cultural white supremacy.

INCARNATIONAL EMBODIMENT

For centuries, Black women laid the foundation for their shared political solidarity and subversion. Embodied in their lives and renarrations, we have seen that women like Maria W. Stewart refused the crumbs from the prejudiced table of patriarchy and patterned their narratives after the Hebrew prophets and New Testament figures, like Mary, the mother of Jesus. The latter announce, through their narrative embodiment, Jesus's solidarity with the dispossessed. In life, as with the prophetic forebearers, prophets defeat oppression not through tolerance, niceties, and respectability but through reimagining the world in a way that topples oppressors and exalts victims.

Such reimagining in the Bible often takes on a scandalous tone, one that subverts embodied hierarchies of gender and class expectations. For example, Beth Allison Barr notes, "By allowing a woman to anoint him with oil, Jesus overturns male headship—allowing a woman to do what only men had been able to do until that moment: anoint the king."[45] The woman in this anointing narrative remains nameless not because of patriarchal presumptions within the text but because by remaining nameless, the individual woman serves as an invitation to all women. This allows for what Robert J. Patterson calls the "typological" renarration seen in womanist biblical interpretation—a renarration that invites Black women to identify with the various biblical characters: "By typologically identifying with female biblical figures that include Mary (the mother of Jesus), Jochebed (Moses's mother), Hagar (Ishmael's mother), and Queen Esther (King Ahasuerus's wife), black women 'wrote defiantly or pleadingly, prayerfully or confidently, testifying to their lives and testing the ability of language and their readers to convey and to understand the truths that—from the depths of their experiences—they knew.'"[46]

Patterson's use of "typological" misses the fulness of what womanist hermeneutics does. Black women do not merely see themselves as types. They see themselves as *incarnations*, *embodiments*, or *heirs* of these prophetic traditions. Throughout her autobiography, Julia Foote "expands the notions of both 'Word' and 'body'. . . . Her calling was to help people say yes to God by bodying the Word of God to them."[47] According to Kate Hanch, such bodying of the Word entails defying the secular-sacred binary because religious experience is never separable from *bodily* experience: "To body the Word specifically is to claim that bodies engaged in the act of proclamation are holy, sacred bodies."[48] Thus, in their hermeneutical identification and embodiment, Black women like Julia Foote "self-consciously invoked biblical narratives in which (Black) women rebelled against oppressive institutions, led communities, and triumphed in the face of adversity, in order to destabilize biblical authority as the chief arbiter of their civil disenfranchisement."[49] Additionally, they claim divine authority, claim vivification of the prophetic spirit. They do not merely establish their moral claims on the Bible but, like the Hebrew prophets, establish their claims on their experience of the Holy Spirit who spoke to the prophets in the Bible.

REDEMPTIVE SELF-LOVE

James H. Cone argues that theology as a discipline fails to appreciate the liberative angles introduced by Black theology and, implicitly, by womanist theology because theology still works with white Western notions of soteriology.[50] Therefore, he says, we never ask the simple question, "What are the theological implications of God's love for the black person in America?"[51] White theology and rhetoric loses the ability to articulate Black humanity without an adequate awareness of God's redemptive love for Black people. In this section, we examine the various ways Julia Foote discursively demonstrates her acceptance and assertion of God's redemptive love and therefore the place of Black women within the human community. I begin by discussing self-love and the subversive elements of Foote's doctrine of entire sanctification. Then, I address Foote's use of apocalyptic imagery as an affirmation of self-love. From there, I discuss Foote's reinterpretation of the Eve narrative from Genesis 3 as an expression of self-love that liberates all women. Finally, I discuss the movement from victim to victor in Foote's cleansing encounter with Christ.

SELF-LOVE AND SUBVERSIVE SANCTIFICATION

Strains of nineteenth-century white theology questioned whether Black people had souls. Certain ecclesial authorities argued that if they did not have souls, chattel slavery carried no ethical consequences. However, even if they did have souls, to these theologians, those souls had earned enslavement. "Traditionally, the Negro had been considered a kind of 'Canaanite, a man devoid of Logos,' whose low social status was 'a punishment resulting from sin or from a natural defect of the soul.'"[52] Even the Methodist Episcopal Church had treated Foote's parents not "as Christian believers, but as poor lepers" whose spiritual status sat below anyone with white skin.[53]

The Wesleyan doctrine of entire sanctification supplied a subversive strand of spirituality that not only countered the claim that Black people lacked souls but went so far as to proclaim that those souls stood worthy of love from God, neighbor, and self:

Wesleyan Methodism constructed a more benevolent God and a more democratic means of redemption than Puritanism did, positing that salvation was achieved through Grace alone. The Methodist conversion relation, then, detailed how the Christian transformed her life from one of sin to one of sanctification. Methodist theology, then, was one of personal transformation. To be sure, black Christians were drawn to the requirement that the conversion narrator, creed notwithstanding, should testify to God's intervention in the sinner's life, for they perceived it as a worthy rejoinder to the whites' theory that the Christian God did not esteem Africans as full—as opposed to 'three-fifths'—human beings.[54]

In other words, Wesleyan theology, with its stress on sanctification as an essential aspect of the *ordo salutis*,[55] offered an opportunity for Julia Foote and her contemporaries to grow in redemptive self-love and see themselves as authoritative interpreters of the Bible.[56] This combination of redemptive self-love and entire sanctification matters to our discussion of Foote's call narrative because through her acceptance of and emphasis on entire sanctification (which she sometimes calls "holiness" or "perfection"), Foote receives her call to preach. The former necessarily precedes the latter.

Entire sanctification in the Wesleyan tradition has as much to do with redemptive love for God, neighbor, and self as it does with the abstinence from specific actions (alcohol, gambling, sex, etc.). While holiness has a widespread association with abstinence, in Wesleyan theology, abstinence provides only one half of the equation; the other half of holiness has to do with progress in the virtues of holy love. As John Wesley explains, "It is that habitual disposition of soul which, in the sacred writings, is termed holiness; and which directly implies, the being cleansed from sin, 'from all filthiness both of flesh and spirit'; *and, by consequence*, the being endued with those virtues which were also in Christ Jesus; the being so 'renewed in the spirit of our mind,' as to be 'perfect as our Father in heaven is perfect.'"[57]

Those who receive entire sanctification do not simply cease to sin; they receive freedom to pursue virtue and live lives of holy love. In both abstaining from and receiving freedom, "sanctification was thought of as a state of complete spiritual purification and perfection,"[58] with profound implications for women like Julia Foote: "Belief in the Wesleyan version of sanctification freed them to trust the prompting of their innermost selves because of their conviction that what came from within was of the Holy Spirit, not the corrupt ego. Thus, these . . . women exhibited in their lives and their writing a remarkable sense of self-worth, self-confidence, and power, despite the traditional spiritual autobiography's treatment of the self as a deceiving antagonist."[59]

Foote knew her desire to fulfill God's call to preach inevitably invited the indignation of patriarchal Christian authority. Her embrace of entire sanctification and its implicit invitation toward self-love enabled her to counter her own reticence and that of her familiar and ecclesial naysayers. To self-worth and self-confidence, the womanist might rightly add redemptive self-love.

Because Foote experiences entire sanctification—a perfecting of the soul that aligns her with divine will—those who question her call become the adversaries of holiness and therefore God. Still, she begins with herself. She acknowledges that she had, without warrant, always prohibited female preaching. While likely true, the rhetorical effect of this statement and her general unwillingness (it takes four angelic appearances and a vision of the Trinity to convince her to preach) bolster her argument against those who oppose her preaching. By citing her own ignorance, impotence, and disinclination, she cuts the audience's objections out from under them before they can wield them against her. No critic can prove more critical than Foote. She did not choose the prophetic burden; God placed it on her.[60] Sanctification compelled her submission to God more than her submission to man.

Her husband having already expressed hesitance over her holiness teaching, her pastor, Jehiel C. Beman, became the primary opponent to Foote's preaching. When she initially informed him of her call, he rejoined that she would realize her error when she attained more spiritual maturity.[61] He later lamented Foote's leadership among the laity, accused her of attempting to split the church with her holiness doctrines, and threatened excommunication upon any church that invited her to preach. Undoubtedly, he understood and had a distaste for the democratic undertones of her sanctification experience.[62] Still, his rejection—and the denominational silence around his abusive behavior—had a profoundly negative social and psychological impact on Foote. She eventually left Boston for the more hospitable Philadelphia. William H. Myers highlights this in his analysis of contemporary call narratives and the desire for communal affirmation: "What the callees desire most is help understanding the experience. Therefore, people who know something about this kind of experience are sought out, whether they are relatives or not. . . . The people they choose to tell vary. The person most frequently told is the pastor," and "rejection by the pastor makes it most difficult for the callee to get sanctioned in the community."[63]

Regardless of her pastor's resistance, Julia Foote, after her heavenly visitation, represents herself as "serenely confident, as a result of [her] 'sanctification' by the Holy Spirit."[64] She responds to Beman's sneers and insults of her intelligence and education with diminutive ire: "My gifts are very small, I know, but I can no longer be shaken by what you or anyone else may think or say."[65] She later adds, "Man's opinion weighed nothing with me, for my commission was from heaven, and my reward was with the most high."[66]

We ought not overlook the rhetorical power of these affirmations of self-love and spiritual authority. For example, when Black spiritual autobiographies begin with the announcement "I was born," they affirm the humanity of the rhetor in a social context that denies their humanity from the beginning of life. The story that follows "I was born," establishes how they reclaimed their humanity and learned to love themselves despite their context. If simple statements such as "I was born" carry the weight of the rhetor's humanity, how much more weight does it carry when a Black woman declares God told her, "You are now prepared, you must go where I have commanded you"[67] or proclaims back to her pastor, "I can no longer be shaken by what you or anyone else may think or say."[68] In these affirmations of her humanness and calling, she affirms her experience of sanctification and restoration to the divine image. As such, she retains the capacity to hear and respond to the divine voice as well as any man. She retains the capacity to receive divine love and love herself regardless of white supremacy or patriarchy in the Black church.[69]

THE APOCALYPTIC GENRE

Most people, including scholars, outside biblical studies assume the apocalyptic genre has an escapist bent motivated by end-times anxiety. This assumption primarily arises from an almost-exclusive rhetorical analysis of privileged white eschatology, as seen in the escapist narratives of evangelical and fundamentalist Rapture theology. While the electoral clout of white eschatological escapism has necessitated this emphasis, it has created an opening in our discipline, especially when reading women like Julia Foote. Not a diversionary doctrine driven by white middle-class fear, apocalyptic rhetoric has historically been produced by marginalized communities looking for an "unveiling" of divine purposes in their suffering. Indeed, the genre contains futuristic images of divine wrath and the destruction of oppressors, but these notions remain secondary to the highly visualized, dramatic revelation of God's intentions for the oppressed community.

Rodney H. Jones says that genres link people together and link people with specific activities, identities, roles, and responsibilities.[70] Both in the biblical apocalyptic genre and African American apocalyptic genre, the audience's desired activity, identity, roles, and responsibilities are precisely what the apocalyptic genre attempts to shape. It utilizes heavenly, visionary, sometimes future-oriented[71] rhetoric to make the audience a certain kind of person, such as liberated, just, imaginative, prophetic. Barry Brummett captures this idea well in his analysis of apocalyptic rhetoric:

> [Apocalyptic rhetoric] is a mode of thought and discourse that empowers its audience to live in a time of disorientation and disorder by revealing to them a fundamental plan within the cosmos. Apocalyptic is that discourse that restores order through structures of time or history by revealing the present to be a pivotal moment in time, a moment in which history is reaching a state that will both reveal and fulfill the underlying order and purpose in history.[72]

Brummett rightly accents the revelatory rather than the wrathful, futuristic, or escapist aspects of the apocalypse.

Similarly, David Bobbitt and Harold Mixon's essay on the apocalyptic rhetoric of Doctor King carefully disassociates apocalypse and pessimism. They suggest four alternative characteristics: apocalyptic rhetoric (1) involves a perception of crisis and (2) is recounted as a narrative, and it is (3) deterministic and (4) transcendent.[73] By *deterministic* they mean apocalyptic rhetoric expresses "the inevitable culmination of the plan of God."[74] For them, apocalyptic rhetoric has a future orientation that minimizes human political involvement. However, they miss that the objective of the future-oriented aspect of King's apocalyptic rhetoric lies precisely in motivating the present hearers to take advantage of this moment: "*Now* is the time to rise from the dark and desolate valley of segregation to the sunlit path of racial justice. *Now* is the time to lift our nation from the quicksands of racial injustice to the solid rock of brotherhood."[75]

As a doubly oppressed person, Julia Foote applies apocalyptic imagery from the position of marginality. Her subgenre choice of an apocalyptic narrative displays the present or realized divine plan that transcends the crisis of white supremacy and patriarchy.[76] The prospect of the apocalypse does create some anxiety in Foote, but it acts more as a reminder of God's abiding presence, advocacy, attentiveness, and action to redeem the world and deliver the chosen people through their time of trial. Like her use of spiritual autobiography, her use of apocalyptic genre as a subgenre within the spiritual autobiography reminds her readers—mainly, the insiders to her protowomanist holiness community—of God's ongoing activity in the present. Her apocalyptic rhetoric aims to liberate the minds and bodies of her audience. It contains no hint of escapist or diversionary intentions. The appearance of angels, the vision of a restored Eden, and images of a sea of converts all motivate a this-worldly response from Foote. She does not employ apocalyptic rhetoric for escape, but rather engagement. She employs the apocalypse as a means of assuring her audience of God's redemptive love lavished on her and proclaimed through her prophetic discourse. Her renarrating of Eve's story exhibits a concrete application of the apocalyptic genre.

A SECOND EVE

Whereas white patriarchal hermeneutics habitually attempt a kind of privileged impartiality and objective distance from biblical texts, Black church hermeneutics have embraced the subjectivity of the Black experience when reading the Bible. Rejecting white individualism and privatized spirituality as universal hermeneutical grids, the Black church has often interpreted the Bible through a collectivist, communitarian, political lens. More, they read the Bible by placing themselves in the center of the story of divine deliverance, making themselves subjects and agents in the story rather than objects "over" the narrative. Kimberly P. Johnson notes that this subjective entrance into the text permits women, particularly Black women, to aggressively destroy destructive female images and linguistic violence stemming from biblical text as well as from popular, privileged readings.[77]

As a protowomanist, Foote offers an enchanting example of this hermeneutic. In her climactic vision, the angelic intermediary escorts her to a heavenly realm where she sees a tree with branches so large she cannot see its ends. After an encounter with the divine Trinity and a walk to the shore, the angel returns her to this tree. This time, "it hung full of fruit" she had not previously noticed.[78] Having received divine commissioning and cleansing, she can discern things she could not previously detect. The Holy Spirit plucked some of the tree's fruit and handed it to her. She sat down and ate it. It tasted like no fruit she had ever eaten.

When the vision begins, the tree has an apocalyptic kind of hyperbolic symbolism: it unveils (in terms of the meaning of *apocalypse* as *unveiling*) the reign of God extending an unfathomable length. The tree reminds a biblically informed reader of the Tree of Life in Revelation 22 with its twelve different fruits and cosmic healing properties. This connection grows stronger when we consider, in conjunction with this tree, Revelation 22 promises the servants of God a vision of God's face, which Foote receives in this encounter.

In the second encounter with the tree, Foote fills the tree with apocalyptic significance and douses it with redeemed Edenic significance. In Genesis 3, Eve, in an absence of divine approval, initiated taking the forbidden fruit from the Tree of the Knowledge of Good and Evil.[79] After Eve plucks fruit from the tree, she gives some to her husband, who eats with her. Foote employs this Edenic imagery by casting herself as a second Eve. Not only does this second Eve have divine approval, but also the Holy Spirit plucks the forbidden fruit (of preaching) from the tree and *gives* it to her. Foote, the second Eve, does not *take* the fruit without permission; she receives it as a gift to enjoy and savor. She receives divine authority to preach not by thievery of forbidden fruit but by divine imperative and will. Whereas Eve gave the fruit to her husband, and he also ate without permission, Foote, in the absence of her husband, receives sustenance from the very Spirit of God.

In reinterpreting the Edenic imagery and employing an alternative hermeneutic that seeks to unshackle women from destructive feminine images and linguistic violence in the Bible, Foote reframes the narrative such that Eve and all women with her now find redemption. No longer of her own initiative (Foote, after all, expressed quite a bit of reticence), Eve has now received divine permission, affirmation, and love to proclaim the redemptive story of this tree and its message of the endless reign of God. No longer the temptress or the Jezebel, through womanist hermeneutics, God restores Eve to her place of submission to the divine Trinity (as opposed to male authority) and her mission of publicly proclaiming divine deliverance to all humanity (as opposed to doing domestic or support work).

Redemptive self-love means rereading the Bible in a way that highlights God's redemptive love for women rather than reading in a way that subjects women to endless submission and secondary status. It means restoring women to their original place of equality with men. Such a reading entails reinstating Black women to their original place of equality with whites. At one time, God inhibited Adam's race from having access to the Tree of Life by placing an angel with a flaming sword outside Eden. Julia Foote, a second Eve, now regains that access to the Tree of Life through an angelic mediator, a commission of the Father, a gift of the Spirit, and a washing of the Son.

FOOTE WASHING

Elaine M. Flake reminds us that womanist preaching's ability to reach the hearts, minds, and souls of African American women hinges on its hermeneutic and its facility to "employ an analysis of Scripture that reconstructs the Word of God in ways that are liberating to women as well as men and that reflects the totality of the African American experience."[80] In particular, for Flake, the Black church has hindered Black women's liberation because of a default patriarchy. For Flake, dismantling this patriarchy entails, among nine other things, an interpretation of the Bible that posits Jesus as an advocate and friend of Black women.[81] As a protowomanist, Julia Foote's call narrative and visionary experience provide a perfect example of a Christological hermeneutic of advocacy. Foote's encounter with Christ moves her from victim to victor, reversing generations of abuse and victimization. Jesus takes her by the hand, strips her of her clothing, and cleanses her, all acts of affection and approval.[82]

A straightforward intertextual interpretation of Foote's encounter with Jesus, where Jesus cleanses her, reminds the reader of John 13, where Jesus washes his disciples' feet. Contextually, Christ confirms his affection for his disciples even though their faith falters, and they deny him at his arrest. With this textual connection in place, Foote places herself in the role of an apostle, whom John says Jesus "loved . . . unto the end."[83] Foote's identification with these loved ones and their apostolic offices adds another layer to her redemptive self-love. Because Christ loves her, she can love herself even in her wavering faith. Sallie M. Cuffe states that such rhetorical moves—which identify African American women with New Testament apostolic personalities—function to liberate their identity and establish their autonomy as Black women "birthed and commissioned by a faith conversion" and, indeed, by direct calling.[84]

Further, in appealing to John 13, Foote not only claims herself as an apostle who received a cleansing just as the original disciples did but also casts her pastor and other naysayers in the role of either Judas or Peter. If they persist rejecting Foote's calling, they analogically align with Judas; if they repent and embrace Foote's calling, they fall in the category of restored Peter. As a protowomanist, Foote concerns herself with the redemptive love of God for the entire community. Anyone willing to embrace her message can find restoration.

However, something more happens in Foote's encounter with Christ than merely an intertextual reference to John 13. Foote's community transcends her immediate audience; it includes her ancestors. Jesus's advocacy for Foote must redeem not only the present community but also the suffering of the historic community of Black women. It must address systemic and generational violence against Black women's humanity. Because of this larger understanding of community, we should read Jesus's washing of Foote in light of her earlier story about an enslaver beating her mother and washing the wounds with "strong salt water" because she refused to submit.[85] The one who beat her also washed her wounds. Then, when her shirt stuck to her back, the enslaver's wife ripped the shirt off so hard that skin came with it.

Like her mother, Foote had struggled to submit to Jesus.[86] However, unlike her mother's enslaver, Jesus advocates for Foote's flourishing. Rather than strong salt water, Jesus washes her with warm, soothing water. Every aspect of the sensual narrative moves Foote and the community of Black women from victims to victors through the cleansing act of Jesus. It reverses the generational wounds inflicted on her mother and others. Thus, the narrative is full of meaning: it presents Jesus as an advocate and friend of women, it addresses violence on a systemic and generational level, it intertextually mimics the foot-washing scene of John 13, it validates Foote's apostolic claims, and, most significantly, because of this imagery, Foote, her audience, and her ancestors can now experience redemptive self-love.

CONCLUSION

Tamura Lomax argues that while cultural criticism of Black feminism offers unique insights into cultural production and subversive rhetoric, scholars need to do further work on the stories of Black women and girls who stake their identity and purpose in life in Christian belief. Thus, we need a more sustained engagement that "explores the significance of Christianity, and specifically the Black Church, in Black America and diasporic women's and girls' lives."[87] This chapter on Julia Foote has sought to do just that by placing her not merely within the Black prophetic tradition but within the biblical narrative. Julia Foote asserted her humanity and thereby made virtuous Black women's self-love via religious rhetoric that can "flex and adapt" with the messiness of *embodiment* and incarnation.[88] With narrative as her "weapon of choice, [she] literally battled for the souls and humanity of black people in nineteenth-century society while opposing racial and gender discourses being promulgated by the colonial hegemony."[89]

This chapter has argued that Foote functions as a protowomanist who chiefly concerns herself with centering the voices of Black women in discourses of knowledge and productions of power. Later womanists built their notions of redemptive self-love on the prior work of women like Foote, who established her *humanness* via the subversive use of the dominant culture's genres (spiritual autobiography), drew logical conclusions from the dominant culture's doctrines (entire sanctification), applied apocalyptic imagery for the benefit of marginalized communities, and utilized a hermeneutic that reimagined texts traditionally used to promote violence against women (the story of Eve) in a way that directly redeemed both her own story and also those of her ancestors (via Jesus's foot washing).

Foote's employment of such strategies not only reinforced her own redemptive self-love but made Black women's experiences virtuous. It wove a narrative of divine love and self-love that expanded beyond her and her

ancestors to redeem all Black women. Not merely a system of religious doctrines and beliefs, Foote's faith provided "a conceptual framework for living
everyday life,"[90] just as faith continues to provide a framework for millions
of Black women to survive in a world of white supremacy and patriarchy.
Foote functioned as a protowomanist, a prophet of deliverance, a supplanter
of ideologies, and a planter of redemptive self-love.

CHAPTER 4

The Call Narrative of Nat Turner

IDENTIFICATION, INSURRECTION, AND
IMITATING CHRIST

By this time, having arrived to man's estate, and hearing the scriptures commented on at meetings, I was struck with that particular passage which says: "Seek ye the kingdom of Heaven and all things shall be added unto you [Matthew 6:33]." I reflected much on this passage, and prayed daily for light on this subject—As I was praying one day at my plough, the spirit spoke to me, saying, "Seek ye the kingdom of Heaven and all things shall be added unto you." Question—what do you mean by the Spirit[?] Ans. The Spirit that spoke to the prophets in former days—and I was greatly astonished, and for two years prayed continually, whenever my duty would permit—and then again I had the same revelation, which fully confirmed me in the impression that I was ordained for some great purpose in the hands of the Almighty. Several years rolled round, in which many events occurred to strengthen me in this my belief. At this time I reverted in my mind to the remarks made of me in my childhood, and the things that had been shewn me—and as it had been said of me in my childhood by those by whom I had been taught to pray, both white and black, and in whom I had the greatest confidence, that I had too much sense to be raised, and if I was, I would never be of any use to any one as a slave. Now finding I had arrived to man's estate, and was a slave, and these revelations being made known to me, I began to direct my attention to this great object, to fulfil the purpose for which, by this time, I felt assured I was intended. Knowing the influence I had obtained over the minds of my fellow servants, (not by the means of conjuring and such like tricks—for to them I always spoke of such things with contempt) but by the communion of the Spirit whose revelations I often communicated to them, and they believed and said my wisdom came from God. I now began to prepare them for my purpose, by telling them something was about to happen that would terminate in fulfilling the great promise that had been made to me—About this time I was placed under an overseer, from whom I ran away—and after remaining in the woods thirty days, I returned, to the astonishment of the negroes on the plantation, who thought I had made my escape to some other part of the country, as my father had done before. But the reason of my return was, that the Spirit appeared to me and said I had my wishes directed to the things of this world, and not to the kingdom of Heaven, and that I should return to the service of my earthly master—"For he who knoweth his Master's will, and doeth it not, shall be beaten with many stripes, and thus have I chastened you." And the negroes found fault, and murmured against me, saying that if they had my sense they would not serve any master in the world. And about this time I had a vision—and I saw white spirits and black spirits engaged in battle, and the sun was darkened—the thunder rolled in the Heavens, and blood flowed in streams—and I heard a voice saying, "Such is your luck, such you are called to see, and let it come rough or smooth, you must surely bare it." I now withdrew myself as much as my situation would permit, from the intercourse of my fellow servants, for the avowed purpose of serving the Spirit more fully—and it appeared to me, and reminded me of the things it had already shown me, and that it would then reveal to me the knowledge of the elements, the revolution of the planets, the operation of tides, and changes of the seasons. After this revelation in the year 1825, and the knowledge of the elements being made known to me, I sought more than ever to obtain true holiness before the great day of judgment should appear, and then I began to receive the true knowledge of faith. And from the first steps of righteousness until the last, was I made perfect; and the Holy Ghost was with me, and said, "Behold me as I stand in the Heavens"—and I looked and saw the forms of men in different attitudes—and there were lights in the sky to which the children of darkness gave other names than what they really were— for they were the lights of the Saviour's hands, stretched forth from east to west, even as they were extended on the cross on Calvary for the redemption of sinners. And I wondered greatly at these miracles, and prayed to be informed of a certainty of the meaning thereof—and shortly afterwards, while laboring in the field, I discovered drops of blood on the corn as though it were dew from heaven—and I communicated it to many, both white and black, in the neighborhood—and I then found on the leaves in the woods hieroglyphic characters, and numbers, with the forms of men in different attitudes, portrayed in blood, and representing the figures I had seen before in the heavens. And now the Holy Ghost had revealed itself to me, and made plain the miracles it had shown me—For as the blood of Christ had been shed on this earth, and had ascended to heaven for the salvation of sinners, and was now returning to earth again in the form of dew—and as the leaves on the trees bore the impression of the figures I had seen in the heavens, it was plain to me that the Saviour was about to lay down the yoke he had borne for the sins of men, and the great day of judgment was at hand. About this time I told these things to a white man, (Etheldred T. Brantley) on whom it had a wonderful effect—and he ceased from his wickedness, and was attacked immediately with a cutaneous eruption, and blood oozed from the pores of his skin, and after praying and fasting nine days, he was healed, and the Spirit appeared to me again, and said, as the Saviour had been baptised so should we be also—and when the white people would not let us be baptised by the church, we went down into the water together, in the sight of many who reviled us, and were baptised by the Spirit—After this I rejoiced greatly, and gave thanks to God. And on the 12th of May, 1828, I heard a loud noise in the heavens, and the Spirit instantly appeared to me and said the Serpent was loosened, and Christ had laid down the yoke he had borne for the sins of men, and that I should take it on and fight against the Serpent, for the time was fast approaching when the first should be last and the last should be first. Ques. Do you not find yourself mistaken now? Ans. Was not Christ crucified. And by signs in the heavens that it would make known to me when I should commence the great work—and until the first sign appeared, I should conceal it from the knowledge of men—And on the appearance of the sign, (the eclipse of the sun last February) I should arise and prepare myself, and slay my enemies with their own weapons. And immediately on the sign appearing in the heavens, the seal was removed from my lips, and I communicated

the great work laid out for me to do, to four in whom I had the greatest confidence, (Henry, Hark, Nelson, and Sam).

—THOMAS R. GRAY AND NAT TURNER, *THE CONFESSIONS OF NAT TURNER*[1]

Before the Great Awakening, white Christian enslavers expressed minimal interest in converting enslaved Africans to Christianity.[2] Some of this
indifference initially stemmed from their supposition that enslaved persons
lacked fully human qualities. Most of their reluctance, however, arose from
the egalitarian threads embedded within the biblical narrative. No matter the
number of hierarchy-sustaining proof texts they employed, enslavers always
sensed a latent liberationism lurking within the biblical text.[3] One need not
believe in *nommo*-related word magic to see that calling an enslaved person
"brother" or "sister" subversively speaks equality into existence.

The religious revivals during the Great Awakening had a significant impact
on the system of slavery. While it took a civil war to unshackle enslaved
peoples, the Great Awakening provided modes of resistance previously
unrecognized or employed. For example, after the Great Awakening, "mission societies were set up to instruct Africans in the doctrines of Protestant
Christianity,"[4] which gave Black and white Christians a common theo-ethical
vocabulary. Further, given Protestant Christianity's emphasis on the biblical
text, reading became an aspect of the conversion process for some enslaved
persons, opening a world of possibilities for revolution both within and
without the religious sphere. Indeed, even those enslaved persons who never
had the opportunity to read, the Great Awakening's Protestant revivalist bent
emphasized an experience-driven, rather than doctrine-driven, religiosity.
By emphasizing conversion experiences, Great Awakening evangelists "made
Christianity more accessible to illiterate slaves,"[5] thereby creating space for
religious experiences outside the orthodoxy of their enslavers. Religious
experience thus provided some of the emotional energy, individual impetus,
and subversive symbolism to resist enslavement and reinterpret both the
Bible and the social order in ways that benefited those enslaved.[6] Thus, the
Great Awakening supplied an ethnically and ethically diverse group of Africans with a shared ethnic identity and ethical framework, which inevitably
threatened institutional slavery and its profiteers.[7]

These revolutionary undercurrents underwrote religion-saturated insurrections throughout the mid-eighteenth and early nineteenth centuries. The
Stono Rebellion (1739),[8] the Prosser Rebellion (1800),[9] the plot of the Vesey

Rebellion (1833),[10] David Walker's 1829 *Appeal to the Coloured Citizens of the World* encouraging rebellion, and Henry Highland Garnet's *An Address to the Slaves of the United States* arguing for the religious responsibility to rebel against enslavers[11] all "galvanized white anxieties" and "linked slave revolt with slave religion."[12]

The role of religion in these revolts coincides with the developing leadership of Black preachers. Particularly in rural communities where "large masses of ignorant, more often illiterate, slaves participated in whatever social and religious relationships, they were allowed, the preacher became one of the most powerful figures in controlling the life patterns of this group of people."[13] They functioned as problem solvers, hope bringers, prophetic energizers, plantation workers, intimate associates with other enslaved people, mediators, and sages. Often in their midlife, they had a reputation for their hard work and calming effect on others. Most importantly, many had a talent for oratory, which when combined with literacy, made regional social contacts possible.[14]

For these preachers, the Bible functioned as a moral and religious source of prophetic energizing, especially for revolt, which "made use of religion both as a pretense for insurgent activity and as a source of moral justification for the uprising itself."[15] Walker's *Appeal*, for example, made use of prophetic rhetoric as a condemnation of white Christianity's moral hypocrisy and apocalyptically condemned enslavers and their enablers to divine wrath. Indeed, *Appeal* had such a reach that when news of Nat Turner's revolt reached the ears of Virginians outside of Southampton, "the governor of that state pronounced the *Appeal* partly to blame" because of Walker's theological and moral contentions that enslaved persons had a Christian duty to obtain freedom by force if necessary.[16]

The connection between Turner and Walker, whether real or imagined, increased enslavers' fears that Turner's "revolt might still grow into a broader insurrection. Their anxiety led to hysteria and violence,"[17] not to mention legal and social fallout.[18] Indeed, Turner's revolt was felt in northern states, such as Maryland, where "all African Americans were forbidden from assembling or attending religious meetings unless the gathering was led by a licensed white clergyman or other respectable white person. Under this scheme religious gatherings would continue, but they were envisioned as happening under close supervision, requiring that white people be present until the close of the meeting and constables break up unsupervised gatherings."[19] Turner's home state of Virginia even "declared it illegal for slave or free blacks to 'preach, exhort, or conduct, or hold any assembly or meeting, for religious or other purposes, either in the daytime or at night.'"[20] Indeed, they further forbade teaching an enslaved person to read or write.

These political and economic realities also created tensions over ecclesial and hermeneutical authority. White Christians responded by using religious instruction as a mechanism of social control,[21] while Black congregants increasingly saw the binary of spiritual egalitarianism and somatic enslavement as irreconcilable. Ecclesial and hermeneutical authority must apply to white and Black people alike no matter the impediments against or implications for enslavers.[22]

I observe these struggles for interpretive authority, as well, in scholastic approaches to Nat Turner's 1831 revolt, the bloodiest slave insurrection in American history. Whereas scholars have appreciated the economic realities encumbering human trafficking in 1831 Virginia,[23] the role of religion in Turner's rebellion often gets discounted or diminished. For example, Daniel S. Fabricant and Seymour L. Gross and Eileen Bender reduce *The Confessions of Nat Turner* to a mere political statement made by Thomas Gray, Turner's attorney. To them, we cannot trust Gray's transcription of Turner's tale because Gray has turned Turner either into a vengeful villain manufactured to vanquish white fear about further slave rebellions[24] or into someone who merely promotes the "interests of the Southern slaveocracy."[25] Even Molefi Kete Asante, who writes extensively about Turner's religious visions, calls him "a man completely controlled by visions and self-persuasion."[26] To him, Turner exploits proof texts from the Bible to prop up his self-anointed messiahship and self-focused hermeneutic. While Asante takes Turner's religion seriously enough to speak of it as the spark of Turner's radicalism, he does not see it as anything other than self-deception and communal opportunism, "and like messianic spirits before and after him, he moved in an *artificial environment, created by his own deception and maintained by that of his followers.*"[27]

Indeed, these interpretations of Tuner make sense. Turner's sanity is preserved in Fabricant's and others' approaches; and Asante's interpretation explains the horrific violence, which feels like it needs justifying. As a history professor once told me, when he teaches the Turner story to his students each semester, they tend to support Turner's insurgency until it is pointed out that Turner and his co-insurrectionists returned to kill the children. It is easier, therefore, to explain away Turner's actions and rhetoric as mere fabrications or the result of an enslaved man's insanity. Still, rhetorically, whereas Fabricant and Gross and Bender see Turner's religious fanaticism as a problem of text versus voice, Asante appears agreeable to accepting that the text transmits Turner's authentic, albeit delusional, voice.[28] Nevertheless, the former group robs Turner of his agency and the latter, his lucidity. Regardless, all we are left with is a villainous Turner, one who, one way or another, plays into the hands of hegemonic interests. As Nikki M. Taylor points out,

"Anytime a member of a marginalized, powerless group is hailed as a hero, an equally powerful counternarrative casts them as a villain. Vilification is, in fact, typical for those who use violence as the means of liberation."[29] That such predictable vilification happens in our scholastic approaches to Turner urges us to revisit this text again to see if there is another way.

Despite scholastic disregard, skepticism, or vilification, neither the historically enslaved persons nor their enslavers discounted religion's role in Turner's rebellion,[30] even if they doubted the truth of Turner's apocalyptic tale. Within months of Turner's trial, the Virginia legislature passed a law banning the teaching of enslaved persons to read or write,[31] banning both free and enslaved Black folks from conducting their own funeral services,[32] and, most significantly, banning them from "preaching or gathering for church service."[33] Even a November 1831 letter from Gov. John Floyd (Virginia) to Gov. James Hamilton Jr. (South Carolina) highlights the role of religion and Black religious leaders in inciting the insurrection. After discussing the religious efforts of abolitionists, such as teaching enslaved persons to read, Floyd writes,

> Then commenced the efforts of the black preachers, often from the pulpits these pamphlets and papers were read—followed by the incendiary publications of Walker, Garrison and Knapp of Boston, these too with songs and hymns of a similar character were circulated, read and commented upon—We resting in apathetic security until the Southampton affair. . . . From all that has come to my knowledge during and since this affair—I am fully convinced that every black preacher in the whole country east of the Blue Ridge was in the secret . . . that their congregations, as they were called knew nothing of this intended rebellion, except a few leading and intelligent men, who may have been head men in the church.[34]

In other words, Floyd sees Black preachers and church elders as key conspirators in a more extensive system of insurrectionary intentions, of which Turner played only one role.

This chapter, therefore, takes Turner's religious claims as seriously as his audience did, seeing his words neither as an elaborate fabrication of Thomas Gray nor as a product of self-delusion. Textual and psychological analysis lay outside our interests. We must struggle with the Turner of the text. Thus, I take Turner's religious rhetoric as constituted by precisely the kind of claims we should expect from a prophetic persona incarnating the biblical storyline and imitating (i.e., embodying) Jesus's prophetic persona for liberationist purposes.

Turner's legacy may endure and evolve in the works of Harriet Beecher Stowe, G. P. R. James, Martin Delany, Thomas Wentworth, William Lloyd Garrison, and William Styron, but it does so as "a myth, as an imagined configuration of convictions, dreams, hopes and fears."[35] This chapter, instead, interprets Turner not as a mythic man but as a man made by myth. We begin by accenting our analysis of *The Confessions of Nat Turner* with Delindus R. Brown and Wanda F. Anderson's concept of *conscious identification*, which provides invaluable insight into Turner's agency maintenance. After delineating my methodology, I address questions of text and voice as *The Confessions'* interaction between Thomas Gray and Nat Turner gives us insight into how Turner's conscious identification concretely worked. Our final efforts explore the conscious identification and imitatio Christi present within the "prophetic-call-narrative" portion of Turner's tale.[36]

RHETORICAL PROPHETIC IDENTIFICATION

Kenneth Burke argues that whenever persuasive efforts occur, the orator and audience must identify with one another and become consubstantial, or in union with each other in some material or symbolic way. Specifically, the speaker secures persuasion by symbolically assisting the audience through audibly naming and associating with qualities held in common interest.[37] The common interest matters for Burke precisely because identification assumes a prior division:

> Identity is affirmed with earnestness precisely when there is division. Identification is compensatory to division. If men were not apart from one another, there would be no need for the rhetorician to proclaim their unity. If men were wholly and truly of one substance, absolute communication would be of man's very essence. . . . For one need not scrutinize the concept of "identification" very sharply to see, implied in it at every turn, its ironic counterpart: division. Rhetoric is concerned with the state of Babel after the fall.[38]

Because of the division between speaker and audience and the necessity of the audience identifying with the speaker, Burke sees the audience as an equal participant in the making of the rhetorical act. Maurice Charland points this out in his discussion of constitutive rhetoric: "[Burke] does not posit a transcendent subject as audience member, who would exist prior to and apart from the speech to be judged, but considers audience members to participate in the very discourse by which they would be 'persuaded.' Audiences would embody a discourse."[39]

For the prophetic tradition, the qualities held in common interest usually involve some shared notion of the *sacred*. As Andre E. Johnson argues, "For a *prophet* to ground herself in anything not recognized as *sacred* by the audience would be to render that message unimportant. This means that the prophet is indeed part of the community fabric and understands the beliefs of the audience."[40] With Delindus R. Brown and Wanda F. Anderson's notion of *conscious identification*, we see that what community participation means for an oppressed rhetor looks different than participation as a member of the dominant discourse.

Brown and Anderson's "A Survey of the Black Woman and the Persuasion Process" builds on—and in some sense, reverses—Burke's identification theory, arguing that Black women employ identification as a means of resisting the oppressor's persuasive efforts.[41] They define identification as "verbal and nonverbal sign-cues that can be substantially associated among persons within an immediate interpersonal or public communicative situation," which occur before the appearance of resistance in a sequential strategy of persuasive appeals.[42] The oppressor offers cues, singling out specific behavioral characteristics and attitudes they desire these women to identify with. Two distinctive varieties of identification occur in the interaction: unconscious and conscious. Unconscious identification occurs when women unconsciously identify with the characteristics or attitudes placed upon them by the oppressor. The oppressor may communicate oppressively, but the woman misses the verbal cues and unwittingly opens herself to the possibility of persuasion.

Conscious identification, however, entails an intentional effort for the woman to understand and interpret the communicative layers and cues coming from the communicator's lips, mainly when they play to the oppressor's favor. Thus, whether the woman identifies with the oppressor's values or asserts her identity vis-à-vis the oppressor, she at least does so consciously. Conscious identification necessitates an exhaustive understanding of the oppressor's symbolic, linguistic, material, and religious universe. The conscious identifier takes advantage of this knowledge and the fixed social roles within the dominant discourse in order to subvert its power and establish new meaning. Only then can opposition occur. Glen McClish notes the consequence of this for dismantling the constructs of power:

> A speaker who demonstrates mastery of the tradition that oppresses
> him as he employs the arguments and *topoi* of his own subculture . . .
> epitomizes both the paradox and the power of the black antebellum

voice. . . . Because they must command the dominant language while critiquing the power relations on which it is based, the combination of diverse forms and strategies—what I have called rhetorical amalgamation—is required to create both fitting and discursive spaces from which to launch their progressive ethic. African-American rhetoric establishes agency not by dismantling the master's house, but by transforming it into something that suits their aims.[43]

Conscious identification creates locales of liberation and resistance because it energizes women to name the truth about the oppressor's actions and invent remedies for the social maladies inflicted on them. In short, when Black women rightly interpret the oppressor's actions and words, they can subversively apply them to their own advantage instead of the oppressor's. Despite the enemy's efforts to rhetorically influence Black women's identity and activities,[44] the conscious identifier now has weapons to ward off the war against her identity, beliefs, and, to a degree, her body.

Depending on the context, resistance may take either a passive or active approach. Passive resistance employs verbal restraint, layering, "tactful, discrete, and diplomatic actions," thereby leaving the resistor relatively invisible.[45] Active resistance, alternatively, asserts one's identity and visibility. It uses hostility, confrontation, and even violence to sway the oppressor's actions, if not their conscience. Either way, for Brown and Anderson, resistance roots itself in creating something new out of the oppressor's repressive rhetoric.

NAT TURNER'S CONSCIOUS IDENTIFICATION

A cursory reading of *The Confessions* confirms Turner's familiarity with the biblical narrative, particularly the prophetic and apocalyptic portions. The Bible provided the hermeneutical grid through which Turner "could make inferences and judgments about the immediate social milieu."[46] However, this hermeneutical grid does not mimic that of white enslavers. Turner's familiarity with the verbal cues and symbolism of white Christianity remains necessary for conscious identification, but his ability to invoke those cues and symbolism to challenge the oppressor's worldview functions as the basis of his resistance.

By appealing to Christian scriptures and apocalyptic imaginations and applying them to himself messianically, Turner's call narrative shows he had the familiarity necessary for conscious identification. In this, he "ironizes the very process of biblical 'interpretation' by reversing ordinary modes of typological reading and rendering [his] own narrative as the typological basis for the interpretation of scripture."[47] In white Christianity, a closed canon closed revelation. In Turner's Christianity, the Holy Spirit willingly inserts new messiahs into narratives that need embodiment and incarnation. The biblical text, rather than closed, becomes radically energizing, pertinent to every contemporary situation, and continuously open to new interpretive potential. "Turner crafted his prophetic leadership by adopting evangelical rhetoric and styles of authority, while rejecting the institutional framework of the church community and the white paternal oversight that framework entailed."[48] In other words, we see the roots for conscious identification and resistance in Turner's hermeneutic.

Turner's choice of the genre of apocalypse offers valuable insight here. While rhetoric scholars often dismiss the this-worldly potential of apocalyptic rhetoric, "it is the Apocalypse that is missing from most evaluations of black religion."[49] Drawing from Kevin Pelletier's work on sentimental apocalypticism, we see that religious violence, more than mere threats of violence without religion, exacerbated the unease of white enslavers.[50] Turner, paralleling the then-two-year-old *Appeal* by David Walker,[51] incarnates the Bible's apocalyptic aspects, which had bred both fascination and fear in white audiences.[52] He alludes to apocalyptic texts from all over the Bible, employing them to his own advantage because "prophecies of a retributive God, in particular, were a familiar source of fear and constituted the most efficient way to politicize terror in the antebellum period."[53] White audiences, aflame with apocalyptic fervor from the Great Awakening, knew and felt the terror of the apocalyptic texts Turner employs. In a hermeneutical maneuver hardly unique to him, Turner knew of the white terror associated with apocalyptic texts and turned it against them through conscious identification. Rather than a genre of escapism,[54] every apocalyptic reference to heavenly battles, heavenly noises, bloody streams and crops, mysterious hieroglyphics, oozing bodies, eclipses, and Spirit-inspired interactions expresses Turner's rhetorical ability to bypass enslavers' objections and appeal directly to divine authority.[55] "When he finally assumes the duty to work on behalf of [this world's] destruction, it is not from private motives but because he must obey the voice of God. . . . [T]he revolt was not the work of corrupt man but a very angry God."[56] Rhetoric scholars cannot understand the Black church, its theology, or its prophets without exploring apocalypse not as escapism (itself a binary between this-worldly and next-worldly religion) but as a kind of this-worldly engagement and even conscious identification leading to resistance.[57] After all, "Turner saw the roots of his revolutionary leadership in his ability to interpret God's word" without the oversight of the oppressor.[58]

Brown and Anderson's methodology may yet provide other insights into Turner's rhetorical strategy. Scholars have wondered why Turner never mentions his wife or her suffering in *The Confessions*. However, if we interpret *The Confessions* as an attempt to resist slavers through conscious identification, mentioning his wife may be rhetorically counterproductive. Mentioning his wife and her suffering might have provided enslavers an opportunity to dismiss Turner as a resentful man seeking revenge. By only appealing to apocalyptic scenes and heavenly visions,[59] he invokes an authority white tyrants cannot easily discard.

Finally, conscious identification may also explain why, as Asante observes, Nat Turner "could conceive no wrong nor commit any crime."[60] It has nothing to do with an "artificial environment" or "his own deception . . . maintained by that of his followers."[61] Instead, Turner's objective lies in turning the white enslavers' rhetoric against them. He wants them to feel, with apocalyptic anxiety, the cosmological, moral, and religious ramifications of slavery. Rhetorically, confessing wrongdoing not only would communicate *un*conscious identification with his oppressors but also could communicates a failure of messianic nerve—a messianic nerve he needed to come through unambiguously in Thomas Gray's transcription.

AUTHOR AND AGENCY: THE PROBLEM OF *THE CONFESSIONS*

The Confessions of Nat Turner, recorded by Thomas Gray, presents us with the problem of author versus agency. The question orbits around how much of Turner's voice authentically arises from within Gray's authorship. We know Gray acted as Turner's amanuensis, but I also acknowledge Turner had no direct agency in how the document turned out. How much credibility does Gray, a white man who owned thirty-three enslaved persons, have as a transcriber of Turner, a formerly enslaved man who was in jail at the time of publication? Did Gray's own political, economic,[62] and social agendas seep into the story?[63] Like many before him, did Turner say publicly what he knew whites wanted to hear?[64] Did Gray arrange and structure *The Confessions* to give authority to his own interpretation of the events?[65]

Anthony Santoro suggests we can sense a scarcity of impartiality in Gray's account precisely because Gray asserts objectivity.[66] For Gross and Bender, *The Confessions* reflects Gray more than Turner. They argue Gray's work primarily aims to assuage the anxiety of white audiences and assure them of the efficacy of the justice system.[67] For them, the religious rhetoric in *The Confessions* reflects nothing more than Gray's intentions to turn Turner into a bloodthirsty, insane man and, therefore, to minimize the perceived seriousness or systemic hazard Turner may have been to the social hierarchy. Nicholas May also minimizes the role of religion in the rebellion when he says, "Despite popular belief in the antebellum South, most slaves were not actually motivated by religion."[68] Notwithstanding the biblical references so explicit through Nat Turner's and others' insurrection tales of enslaved persons, May argues, "the average black participants, even if religious, may have been motivated by other factors. The testimonies of Turner's rebels, for example, include little or no mention of religion or God as an incentive to revolt."[69]

However, the minimization of religion by these scholars may betray a pedagogical predisposition opposed to taking religious impulses seriously. If scholars fail to hear Turner's authentic voice in this text, we cannot merely blame Gray for the cover-up[70] because scholars have also ignored its presence in *The Confessions* and contemporary documents.[71] Kevin Pelletier's words about scholastic interaction with David Walker have relevance for our discussion on Turner:

> By making violence revolutionary and not theological or merely retributive, critics unwittingly temper Walker's incendiary presence by placing him in a tradition in which violence was necessary to preserve the self-evident freedoms that inhere in all persons. . . . Revolutionary violence, then, is not destabilizing or destructive in these views, but normative and constructive of a world where all persons enjoy the rights and privileges of citizenship. . . . As a result of their fixation on the revolutionary, however, scholars have left very little room for discussing the emotionality of those arguments that, like Walker's, are predicated on apocalyptic terror.[72]

Apocalyptic terror runs on the fuel of religious rhetoric. Though contemporary scholars may wish to minimize such rhetoric, even Turner's executioners knew the religious nature of his revolt: "Your only justification is that you were led away by fanaticism."[73] And as noted earlier, the state of Virginia took the religious impulses seriously as well.

Fortunately, some scholars have, however, taken Turner's voice and religious rhetoric more seriously. Eric J. Sundquist, for example, sees *The Confessions* as Turner's final act of resistance to his enslavers. He argues for a Hegelian dialectal movement between Gray and Turner wherein Turner deceives Gray, playing off Gray's religiolinguistic ignorance and desire to assuage his audience's anxiety by depicting Turner as insane (and therefore isolated).[74] Seeing *The Confessions* as a dialectical chess match confirms the importance of conscious identification as an interpretive method: "One can entertain the possibility that Turner consciously played the trickster and that the language of irony and double vision that is often associated with African American rhetorical forms and the liminality of slavery was his vehicle of revelation. The ambivalence of the 'Confessions' arises less in Gray's manipulation of his story than in Turner's own manipulation of his story and in the shocking millenarian revolutionary violence."[75] Nat Turner's knack for consciously identifying with his oppressors' rhetoric was strengthened by the Great Awakening, the reverberations of which could be felt a hundred years later. With no prior parallel in American history, the Great Awakening provided religious and spiritual intimacy in both vocabulary and values. Randolf Ferguson Scully calls Turner's rebellion "an intimate rebellion" because "blacks and whites in southeastern Virginia had come to share religious ideas and institutions on an unprecedented scale due to the dramatic influx of black men and women into evangelical churches."[76] He catalogs these commonalities as follows: (1) an emphasis on lived, emotional experience, (2) a willing subjection to ecclesial oversight, (3) a celebration of baptism, and (4) a process of church discipline.[77] Scully, of course, notes the different ways these commonalities play out in the lives of Black and white people. Nevertheless, however variously applied, the joint religious vocabulary and values provide avenues for conscious identification and resistance. Far from Eugene D. Genovese's "hate-driven mad man,"[78] Turner exemplifies ease with evangelical values and vocabulary, which enabled his spiritual empowerment. Gray's oversight of Turner's rhetorical strategy works to Turner's benefit, allowing his voice to resound more clearly. White anxiety, rather than assuaged, got amplified.

This discussion of author versus voice matters not because the textual tradition or its origins play a primary role in our discussion[79] but because through Turner's conscious identification, his insurrection and prophetic critique get perpetuated with each reading of The Confessions. To secularize Turner's motivations, reduce them to revenge, or to lose them in Gray's pursuit of social tranquility fails to appreciate Turner's distinctively Christian, decidedly political resistance. In this, Turner refuses to allow Gray's audience to excuse themselves from blame or permit them the tranquility of conscience they desire.[80] Through conscious identification, Turner speaks their vocabularies, articulates their values, models white evangelical morality, and verbalizes their continual vulnerability to apocalyptic violence as long as slavery exists.[81] By consciously identifying with and resisting his oppressors, The Confessions ensures Turner's mission of apocalyptic terror both transcends his life and situates him "in the very world [his rhetoric] aims to destroy."[82]

AUTHORSHIP OF TURNER'S DOCUMENT

Given the racial profiling and power maintenance involved in the recounting of confession narratives, we quickly see how Thomas Gray attempts to subvert Nat Turner's voice to one degree or another. After all, "whenever a dominant discourse is used to account for the discourse (or the materiality) of its opposite, it necessarily precludes the one it purports to elucidate."[83] Thus, the authorship of Nat Turner's *Confessions* is not one of lack of record[84] but of distortion and representation. Melbourne S. Cummings comments, "Consequently, rhetorical researchers are faced not only with the task of discovering and placing black orators into the discipline, but of adjusting facts and reevaluating, reassessing, and reinterpreting fundamental methods and procedures of determining standards for critically judging a speech and the speaking situation."[85] Therefore, the researcher in Black rhetoric must evaluate the speech on a different set of standards than intended by the propagandists, politicians, and journalists involved. We must as Herbert A. Wichelns advises, pay attention "to the relation of the surviving texts to what was actually uttered."[86] Herein lies the value of conscious identification for researching Nat Turner. Conscious identification arises from Black scholarship seeking to restore the lost or hidden agency of Black orators. The text of Turner's *Confessions* resounds with heteroglossia, announcing the presence of the voices of Thomas Gray, Nat Turner, and white audiences[87] lusting for artifacts to reinforce Black criminality.[88]

CALL AND CONSCIOUS IDENTIFICATION

Turner commenced his call narrative with neither doubt nor defensiveness. From the "days of my infancy," his ability to speak of events predating his birth and strange markings on his head convinced his parents and community of his prophetic status.[89] Because "the person possessed from youth with the idea of mission is rare,"[90] the certainty of Turner's calling required community confirmation[91] as "only in terms of other people does the individual become conscious of his own being, his own duties, his privileges and responsibilities toward himself and towards other people."[92] However, once confirmed, such a calling had biblical and apocalyptic character. His childhood calling mimicked that of Samuel, John the Baptizer, and Jesus. Turner picked up on and imitated, specifically, Jesus's theological perceptiveness when perplexing temple priests in Luke 2:22–39. On the heels of a politically and socially subversive birth announcement,[93] Jesus's childhood arguments in the Temple presaged his eventual prominence. Imitatively, Turner's childhood prophetic perceptions, incredible intellect, and seemingly supernatural literacy[94] all affirmed Turner "was cut from the best messianic fabric,"[95] equipped from infancy for incarnation, embodiment, and, indeed, insurrection. Rather than the white Jesus of the enslaver's rhetoric, Turner's imitation of Jesus and other biblical figures reveal a resistant theology wherein "black people are the center of their own spiritual universe,"[96] swept up into the story of God's liberation of the oppressed throughout time and place. As with Jesus, so with Turner in that dismantling established doctrine articulated by people with ties to unjust political power functioned as an indispensable aspect of a prophetic theology of resistance rooted in conscious identification.

Turner's gradual grasp of his "divine inspiration" did not lead him to instantly organize an insurgency in the name of the kingdom of heaven. Instead, he initially seemed ignorant of any future insurrection and, instead, entered a period of prayer, fasting, and seclusion that embodied and imitated that of both Moses and Jesus in the desert prior to their going public.[97] However, during a church meeting, Turner "was struck with that particular passage which says: 'Seek ye the kingdom of Heaven and all things shall be added unto you.'"[98] He contemplated and prayed on this passage for some time until one day, at his plow like the prophet Elisha, he received his calling through the Spirit reciting that same passage. By identifying the Spirit as "the spirit that spoke to the prophets in former days,"[99] he not only justifies his own prophetic vocation but also subverts white theology, which says the "spirit that spoke to the prophets in former days" no longer speaks. "To the prophets in former days" paraphrases Hebrews 1, which explicitly ties Jesus to the larger biblical narrative and the stream of messianic prophets in the Hebrew Bible. In these literary allusions, Turner casts himself as the next messiah who embodies the lineage of Moses, the Hebrew prophets, and Jesus. Like his predecessors, Turner "is mission-oriented and feels a moral or suprarational need to stand as the deliverer of the people."[100] Even when Gray asks him whether he feels he made a mistake in his interpretation of his apocalyptic visions, Turner responds by asking, "Was not Christ crucified?"[101] Gray wants to *identify* Turner with mistaken messiahs and malicious malcontents, but Turner turns white religion against him by citing Christ's crucifixion, itself a kind of lynching in the Roman world.[102] Execution does not itself eradicate Turner's messiahship. Instead, it inaugurated a new apocalyptic and eschatological era of revelation[103] wherein Turner and the people he represented, rather than white America, became "united in their sense that the God of Israel was among them in a special way."[104] They swapped the silent god of whiteness for the speaking God of the prophets, who told Turner of his ordination "for some great purpose in the hands of the Almighty."[105]

Over "several years," numerous undisclosed events occurred confirming Turner's calling, teaching him that "I would never be of any service to anyone as a slave."[106] This recognition, combined with the divine revelations, led him to build a following. However, this Jesus-imitating process of disciple making gets interrupted by the appointment of a new overseer from whom Turner eventually escaped for thirty days. His fellow enslaved persons assumed he had escaped and expressed astonishment at his eventual, willing return. Asante says, "he returned to the overseer with the internal conflict between freedom and obedience raging within him."[107] However, Turner did not return of his own volition or internal conflict, but rather "the Spirit appeared to me and said I had my wishes directed to the things of the world, and not to the kingdom of Heaven, and that I should return to the service of my earthly master."[108] Read as conscious identification, Turner's return did not merely reflect obedience to the overseer (unconscious identification), which led to further enslavement, but moreover imitatio Christi and submission to the Spirit, which led to freedom realized in the present *despite* the oppressor's rhetoric. Given the reference to Exodus, when citing the "murmuring" of his fellows, we could even read this portion as Turner's imitation of Moses. He had escaped Egypt only to obey the voice of God and return (Exodus 3) and later liberate the Israelites. Andre E. Johnson further proposes that Turner may have been imitating Hagar, an enslaved woman, who returns to her mistress under God's direction (Genesis 16) after originally escaping the mistress's oppressive household.[109] Regardless of the Exodus-generation-type "murmuring"[110] of his fellows, Turner refused to see himself as an enslaved person beholden to a white man. Instead, as a prophet beholden to the Spirit, he embodied and incarnated God's *eventual* emancipation in the *present* despite his material circumstances. His prophetic task did not lead to the opiated obedience of unconscious identification but to a prophetic engagement of one who had consciously identified and therefore could resist.

Turner became more aggressive in his symbolic resistance when he moved from subtle citations of scripture and random spiritual encounters to violent apocalyptic visions of holy war. Demonstrating familiarity with white Christianity's portrayal of apocalyptic visions as battles between forces of darkness and forces of light, Turner said, "I had a vision—and I saw white spirits and black spirits engaged in battle, and the sun was darkened—the thunder rolled in the Heavens, and blood flowed in the streams—and I heard a voice saying, 'Such is your luck, such you are called to see, and let it come rough or smooth, you must surely bare it.'"[111] White Christians had long depicted Jesus and angelic beings as white-skinned through sermons and art. Their purity contrasted with the "darkness" of evil beings. Turner recognized this history, understood the moral and theological insinuations therein, and turned it on its head. While the quote above does not specify the morality of either the forces of light or darkness, this may serve a con-scious-identification-related purpose. While Turner certainly conveyed Black nationalist religious themes, Jeffrey Ogbonna Green Ogbar goes further than the evidence allows when he says, "contrary to Anglo-Saxon notions of color and morality, the white spirits represented the wicked, vile, and irredeem-ably demonic forces of the universe. Conversely, the black spirits were the virtuous, godly, and beneficent harbingers of freedom and justice."[112] Indeed, Turner's vision had subversive components in that it consciously identified and countered white notions of morality and color. However, contextually, Turner did not differentiate the forces of light and dark by skin color but by whether or not the individual hearer heeded Turner's messianic message. After all, he did not eliminate the possibility that white people could repent, as evidenced by his baptism of Etheldred T. Brantley. Through this, Ogbar's assertion has value in that "his religion . . . was suited to serve as a vehicle of resistance to slavery on a physical level while simultaneously encapsulating a psychological liberation aspect."[113]

While certainly a psychological and rhetorical battle symbolically subvert-ing white Christian theology, this battle between white and black spirits was understood by Turner as a cosmological, mythological, and theological battle for justice. Against the ancient "serpent that was loosened," Turner waged war as "the embodiment of God's *justice and, in a sense, vengeance*, sent to punish the wayward and to warn the sinful."[114] The serpent contextually signified the dominance and ultimate defeat of white supremacy and slavery. Black people became the chosen people; Turner, their messiah, purging the world of the satanic evil of white Christianity. The biblical images of Christ's crucifixion no longer functioned as the rhetorical tools of white oppressors, but through conscious identification with the biblical narrative, Turner found possibilities for liberation within the religion of the enslaver. He refused to adopt the enslaver's hermeneutics and offered instead an interpretive scheme and application of biblical texts that centered Black prophetic insight.

Turner did not, however, only offer these opportunities for salvation to enslaved people. White people needed freedom from their oppressive actions too. Therefore, Turner summoned them to join his messianic movement. Having told Brantley of his apocalyptic visions, the effect was "wonderful . . . he ceased from his wickedness."[115] Brantley thereafter broke out with an oozing skin disease, from which he received healing after much prayer and fasting. Imitating Jesus's healing of men and women with leprosy as a symbol of his arrival of the apocalyptic kingdom, Turner's healing of Brantley invited all who believe to receive his messianic, apocalyptic healing.

After this, the Spirit appeared to Turner and told him, "As the Saviour had been baptized, so should we be also."[116] Turner attempted to obey and baptize Brantley, but the white Christians refused to allow Turner to do this. He and Brantley then went to a local body of water and, in the presence of those who had turned them away, "were baptised by the Spirit."[117] The baptism portion of Turner's call narrative continues the repeated refrain "the Spirit appeared to me" and "the Spirit said."[118] These spiritual communications employed messianic and apocalyptic categories to navigate the tension between offering salvation to whites who repent and warning of condemnation for those who did not. Despite the white Christian refusal to permit Turner to use the church baptistery, the Spirit's prompting provided a path by which Turner could ignore those whites who reviled him. However, it also provided the whites with a living prophetic witness to the possibility of repentance.

Thus, the significance of Turner's baptism of Brantley did not lie strictly in Brantley's conversion but also in the conversion of a white man. Turner baptized a man who could have, with legal rights, owned him. The reversal of expectations in this narrative runs throughout this scandalous act of resistance. Not only did Turner baptize a white man, upending the religious purity hierarchy of whites over Black folks, and not only did Turner do this in the face of a group of disapproving whites, but also Turner's rhetoric invited white people to repent by giving up the power and privilege of their whiteness. He consciously identified the vocabulary and liturgy central to white conversion (baptism) and turned it to his liberative purpose. Like John the Baptist, who baptized Gentiles, not only Jews, Turner baptized whites, not only Black people, thereby undermining all religious hierarchy.

Unlike white people who rhetorically, theologically, and physically rejected his baptism and ecclesial authority, Turner embraced the possibility of white inclusion in his apocalyptic, messianic movement. Like Israel in the book of Joshua, called ultimately to utterly destroy the Canaanites, Turner must wield the sword of his messianic mission. However, like Israel's acceptance of the Canaanite sex worker Rahab, Turner proved more than willing to accept righteous whites who willingly submitted. Such authority has historically belonged to the oppressor. White Christianity had, for centuries, employed the Canaanite genocides in their messianic and colonial agendas. Turner understood the linguistic, rhetorical, and theological maneuvers white Christians made to justify their enslavement of people of color around the world, and he used it against them by applying it to himself.

With this combination of allusions to Canaanite Genocide and apocalyptic rhetoric, Turner ignored church polity, rejected the orthodoxy of enslavers, and resisted paternalistic religion through conscious identification. Twice noting the governing body's disapproval of his baptism, he demonstrated familiarity with their arguments, rejected them, and baptized Brantley anyway. He shrugged off "evangelical conceptions of authority and their relationship to the racial and gendered hierarchies of the evolving American South."[119] His authority originated in a voice from elsewhere, a voice not beholden to white enslavers' social and political arrangements.

This voice from elsewhere finds articulation most clearly in the apocalyptic portions of Turner's call narrative, such as his interpretation of the eclipse. The final, pivotal piece of the call-narrative portion of *The Confessions*—the part that led him to violence—involved the darkening of the sun reminiscent of Joel 2. One reason for Turner's repeated appeals to apocalyptic visions in nature is Black religion's theology of harmonization with the created order.

The greatest power any human being can attain is the acuity to channel the Cosmic Energy provided by Spirit and to manifest that power on the earthly plane of existence by righting the wrongs and injustices created by those who are spiritually lost or misguided. Within African cultures, the greatest power on earth is the ability to create harmony in place of disharmony, order where once where there was chaos.[120]

In apocalyptic symbolism, the darkened sun did not signify a natural phenomenon to appreciate scientifically but rather symbolized creation's upheaval and the need for Turner to recreate harmony and order. In Genesis 1, the sun rules creation; thus, a darkening of the sun indicates a reversal of creation, a return to chaos. Turner interpreted the darkening of the sun as a reversal of the white man's "order." They had argued from Genesis that God ordained whites to rule Black people, but in the scenes in the sky and the dimming of the sun, Turner used conscious identification to reinterpret the order of creation. His insurrection, rather than instigating chaos, thwarted it. Rather than destroying order, the fall of the white man's order allowed for a new, Black-centered world of harmony.

In an imitation of Christ, Turner answered a question with a question, indicating that he doubted the uniqueness of his apocalyptic interpretation of the eclipse. Gray asked Turner at this point if he knew of other conspiracies of slave rebellion. Turner replied, "Can you not think the same ideas, and strange appearances about this time in the heavens might prompt others, as well as myself, to this undertaking?"[121] Thus, like Israel preparing to invade the promised land and destroy all the Canaanites (empowered at one point by a divine display of power over the sun), Turner commenced his own Canaanite genocide by casting the Christian white enslavers in the role of the unbelievers—a war not of a loose cannon or a lone insurrectionary but of a conscious identifier, a man who knew the symbols, rhetoric, language, and cues of his oppressors and used them for his own liberationist purposes.

CONCLUSION

In this chapter, I have argued that rhetorical scholars should continue to engage the intersections of rhetoric, race, and religion, particularly apocalyptic and prophetic rhetoric, as a means of understanding Black resistance in America. I have applied Brown and Anderson's reframing of Burkean identification theory to *The Confessions of Nat Turner* to show that Turner effectively consciously identifies with the enslaver's rhetoric. Expressing thorough familiarity with white Christian beliefs, Turner had the capability to apply biblical texts and theological beliefs for his subversive intentions. In these observations, we take another step away from an antireligion bias that reduces the religious motivations of people like Nat Turner to economic and political concerns. Indeed, the Black religious tradition does not separate secular and sacred motivations.

Additionally, in this analysis, we see the necessity of rethinking our understanding of prophetic and apocalyptic rhetoric not as foretelling or escapist rhetoric but as a rhetoric of this-worldly engagement. Turner did not merely experience opiated visions of another world that satisfied him with the status quo. He acted against his oppressors precisely because prophetic and apocalyptic rhetoric remained relevant to this life.

Conscious identification involves participation in a specific discourse community, even if only for pragmatic benefit. In this analysis of Nat Turner's conscious identification, I have wished to highlight a few important points. First, as rhetoric scholars, we need more attentiveness to the listening that precedes a rhetorical moment. Turner's tale conveys a prior listening to his community, the biblical text, the oppressive community's mythological rhetoric, a possible familiarity with other confessionary and criminalization narratives—potentially, David Walker's *Appeal*—and, of course, Thomas Gray's attempt to subvert Turner's agency. Each of these plays a role in Turner's conscious identification and prophetic resistance.

Second, African American prophetic-call narratives give us profound insight into Black rhetorical theology and liberationist efforts. This chapter has brought these two items together because Turner's prophetic-call narrative highlights his awareness of white Christian rhetorical theology, his sensitivity to the religious rhetoric within his own community, and his attentiveness to the cosmos around him as a rhetorical agent. We cannot understand Turner and his motivations without understanding his calling. And we cannot understand his calling unless we understand what and to whom he listened. He confesses to all that in a document wherein his agency is often lost or questioned.

Finally, our neo-Aristotelian, Greco-Roman emphasis on persuasion may hinder our ability to see how resistance rhetoric works in situations of audience stagnation. For prophetic figures like Turner, martyrdom may encompass the intended effect.[122] Because they know beforehand the unlikelihood of persuasion, prophets understand their own death as the ultimate rhetorical act. Turner remains willing to die for his cause because death displays the message in a way that preserves it in the mind of the reader: "Whatever the motives of the prophet, his value lies in his reception, the quality of the ethos presented to his auditors. Charisma, we are reminded, is only validated when recognized; it is a social phenomenon. And if the recognition of charisma depends on recognition of the quality of the birth, the calling, only in the quality of the death, it stands to reason that sainthood is always posthumous."[123] In some sense, the prophet's life, death, and calling can only find validation after death and by a later community. This point, of course, has been articulated by others in our field before me. Andre E. Johnson has spoken of the pessimistic prophets who encounter intransigent audiences.[124] Edwin Black's *Rhetorical Criticism* also highlights the overly simplistic assessment of speaker-audience causation particularly when failing to account for the moral predispositions of the audience and their resistance to the speaker's virtues.[125] Maurice Charland, further, correctly notes that because "the audience members . . . participate in the very discourse by which they would be 'persuaded,'" an audience affects the speaker and the speech.[126] Prophetic rhetoric, then, helps scholars assess these rhetorical situations by supplying us with speeches where the expected effect remains minimal. Prophets know their audiences are not necessarily free to be persuaded because their prior moral commitments predate and are "logically prior" to persuasion.[127] In short, in assessing speeches from the African American prophetic tradition, we can catch up to Nat Turner and the Hebrew prophets when they say, "Hearing they do not hear, and seeing they do not see."[128] Of all rhetors, prophets know their "duty is to speak to the people, 'whether they hear or refuse to hear.'"[129]

A Perilous Conclusion

I have argued throughout this book that in response to their call narratives, our four figures each *embody* the rhetorical tradition of the biblical prophets who brought otherworldly oratory to intransigent audiences. This final chapter cauterizes various components of this thesis by comparing these figures as a collective and considering what contributions call narratives from the African American prophetic tradition offer us at the intersection of race, rhetoric, and religion. I begin by reorienting prophetic rhetoric and specifically the African American prophetic tradition within the field of communication.

As delineated in biblical studies and rhetoric, prophetic discourse has often taken on the categories defined by white male rhetors or scholars. As noted, James Darsey's *The Prophetic Tradition and Radical Rhetoric in America* argues that both "Old Testament prophecy and the received notion of American virtue . . . [provide] the essential motive for the radicals examined [and] are products of a patriarchal theology that explicitly holds virtuous action in opposition to 'effeminacy.'"[1] However, such a clear conclusion seems forgone when Darsey confines the scope of his criticism to figures who exalt America's virtues and experience America from the position of racial and gendered privilege. After all, rhetors and prophets from the African American prophetic tradition have rarely reified America's virtues. Nor have womanist scholars or rhetoricians championed the patriarchal presumptions of America, white churches, or many Black churches.

PROPHECY CALLS FOR DAMNING PATRIARCHY

Diverging from Darsey, Kerith M. Woodyard describes a "prophetic liberating principle" within both the Bible and the African American prophetic tradition. This principle, the hermeneutical grid of prophetic figures descending from the Hebrew Bible, justifies an academic reevaluation of prophecy's presumed penchant for patriarchy. As prophets cross-examine the ideological constructs of their culture, they characteristically critique systems of dominion and power, like patriarchy. Thus, "to limit the American radical tradition to Euro-American males does an injustice to the radicality of the very biblical tradition that gives rise to the prophetic voice"[2] of figures like Maria W. Stewart, Julia Foote, Nat Turner, and Richard Allen.

Woodyard's investigation into the ideological constructs of our discipline rings prophetic. Indeed, these ideological constructs may encounter intransigent audiences in the academy. After all, a rhetorical genre we struggle to comprehend with neo-Aristotelian tools threatens some of our most time-honored traditions concerning communication's telos. Yet these traditions and thoughts became commonplace when critical studies primarily consisted of white middle-class heterosexual males. Woodyard thus prophetically proclaims the need to rethink our foundational (and foundationalist) assumptions. These include the importance of persuasion and effect and an expansion of effect to include witness, or, as Edwin Black calls it, "the preservation of morally significant events" in the minds of the hearers.[3]

However, this overhaul of our discipline does not mean we must dispense with all the tools we have developed. Instead, I have demonstrated in these chapters that we can revise and remold the tools we have already developed for liberative purposes. Brown and Anderson led the way with conscious identification. I have followed their lead with cluster analysis. Thus, we have arrived at a place where we can adequately reflect on the comparisons, contrasts, and contributions of the African American prophetic tradition and its call narratives as primers for such a remolding and self-reflexivity.

PROPHECY CALLS FOR A REVIVAL OF INTEREST IN RELIGIOUS RHETORIC

One overarching difficulty in studying prophetic rhetoric and prophetic-call narratives arises with scholars attempting to make sense of rhetorical artifacts, auditors, and rhetors who do not share the scholar's worldview. Quentin J. Schultze calls this the "God-Problem" and labels it "one of the most recurring themes in communication studies."[4] This problem gets exacerbated by our discipline's enduring allegiances to Enlightenment assumptions that have deemed religion an "unpopular, potentially even subversive research agenda that called into question the naturalistic assumptions of modernity."[5]

Nor does it help that scholars often see religion as rigid and repressive. Unquestionably, investigating religious rhetoric with a hermeneutic of suspicion has value. However, a merely repressive appraisal of religious language lacks scholastic rigor and reeks of reductionism given that religious rhetoric also empowers, inspires, and frames liberative work within histori-cally oppressed communities, like the Black church. As James H. Cone says, "Christian theology is language about God's liberation of the weak as defined by Scripture in relation to our contemporary situation."[6] Communities like exilic Israel and the nineteenth-century Black church found religious rhetoric ripe with revolutionary rhetoric. Thus, "too many scholars wrongly assumed, given their own secular assumptions or religious ignorance, that deep devo-tion to religious beliefs and communities were all alike—and that it was intellectually wise to divide the world into two camps, namely, the religious folks who ignorantly held on to ancient myths, and the secular intellectuals who saw through such religious cant and advocated for truth and justice."[7]

By disregarding religious rhetoric as a salient site of scholastic inquiry, rhetoric scholars miss a major rhetorical paradigm that could potentially reshape and challenge our understanding of human communication. Con-sider the origins and location of meaning. Whereas critics locate meaning in the text, the interpreter, or the speaker's intentions, religious rhetors some-times originate meaning in divine communication.[8] Meaning is attained not merely through hermeneutical methodology but moreover methodology in conversation with the contemporary situation and the ethical framework through which one hears. For prophetic rhetoric, ethos, pathos, and Logos all labor in both the proclamation and reception of the message.

From a materialist view, rhetorical critics may rightly see God as irrel-evant, nonexistent, or too distant to provide meaning. Humans create mean-ing; they do not receive it. However, Brian Kaylor argues that communication scholars should at least analyze God as a presumed speaker or a member of the audience: "Rhetorical scholars are left with how the rhetor perceives God and the impact of such a belief on the rhetor's message. The fact that God cannot be examined should not discourage scholars from considering the residual effect of a rhetor's belief in God as an audience member."[9] Schultze goes further: "What would the field of communication studies look like if we posited the existence of God as a speech agent? What kind of follow-up questions would we then ask? What refreshing and interesting questions might emerge in our scholarship and teaching?"[10]

Regardless of the individual critic's disposition toward religion, religious rhetoric endures despite the Enlightenment's eager eulogies. For "when the rhetor gestures to God, they pull back the curtain for the scholar to see the world from their vantage point."[11] The theological or nontheological questions critics might have about the existence of the divine or the pos-sibility of divine-human interaction remain secondary to the fact that the rhetorical artifact, the person who produced the artifact, and the audience of the artifact all often assume the reality of the divine and the possibility of direct divine communication and meaning. Thus, "the critic's task is not to discern the divine will, but rather how the rhetor's expectations of divine expectations shapes the message."[12] Therefore, for the sake of understanding our past and thoughtfully perceiving our future, religious rhetoric requires our continued consideration.

Given the clear complexity of this, particularly in a pluralistic world and a discipline that must reevaluate our positionality, Schultze says communication scholars have three options: (1) embrace naturalism while remaining open to the possibility of meaning outside humanly constructed systems of communication; (2) openly accept the possibility of a "holy other" who cannot communicate with us or, at least, rarely does; and (3) affirm theism with all its own mysteries.[13] To Schultze's list, I have employed a fourth option in this book: embrace naturalism and the lack of a possibility for meaning outside humanly constructed systems of communication while taking seriously the rhetorical impact of the fact that the rhetor and/or audience maintain a theistic worldview. In this, the critic need not remain open to the possibility of meaning outside of human constructs and symbolism. Rather, she commits to meaning as a purely human creation (thus taking the historical, social, and rhetorical situation seriously) while appreciating that the orator and audience do not operate with the same assumption.

This approach benefits rhetorical critics because it asks for self-reflexivity from the scholar and inhibits early judgments on the rhetors. It invites scholars to see that while they may consider the Bible an oppressive text, they allow their subjects to find liberation within its pages. After all, given what we know about the specified prophetic figures' reliance on the biblical text, Monika R. Alston-Miller rightly notes, "accepting the Bible as a patriarchal text that has been appropriated to oppress women can lead to rejecting it (and texts that include it) too quickly, which removes it from the women who used the Bible to marshal arguments against patriarchy."[14]

Further, when rhetoric scholars appreciate how religious rhetoric works, it provides more critical tools for launching effective rebuttals that make sense within the language world of the worshipper. Scholars need not adopt a theistic view before analyzing religious rhetoric in this approach. They simply need to take seriously religious rhetoric's multifaceted material impact in history and the context of their rhetorical artifact.

Indeed, through inquisitiveness and curiosity regarding religious rhetoric, rhetoric scholars can return to the discipline's religious rhetorical roots: "This viewpoint is held in common by Plato and Aristotle, as well as by

thinkers such as Descartes. . . . The tradition I call classical includes all
those who believe that by means of self-evidence, intuition—either rational or empirical—or supernatural revelation, the human being is capable
of acquiring knowledge of immutable and eternal truths, which are the
perfect and imperfect reflexion of an objective reality."[15] Then, a study of
religious rhetoric has both ancient and (post)modern aspects. It takes
the social, economic, political, and racial components of the rhetorical
artifact seriously while acknowledging, at the very least from the rhetor's
perspective, that meaning, truth, and, indeed, words can originate "from
elsewhere." Prophetic rhetoric and call narratives call for more investigation
into these alternatives, possibilities, and modifications of our discipline's
ideological underpinnings.

PROPHECY CALLS FOR AN AWARENESS OF
ALTERNATIVE INFLUENCES ON AMERICAN RHETORIC

Despite decades of critique, academic disciplines continue to work with
Enlightenment tools and binaries from an era when women, persons of color,
and non-Westerners did not have a seat at the table. While having its own
interactions with the Enlightenment and modernity, the Black church was
primarily forged in the fires of slavery and found liberation and resistance
possible via the texts of the Hebrew Bible. Indeed, its use of the Bible highlights the larger formative contributions of the Hebrew Bible on American
rhetoric at large. James Darsey underscores this:

> A view of the American tradition that sees only its mundane and
> businesslike side, that stresses its origins in the Enlightenment, might
> be accused of stressing Locke to the exclusion of Calvin, thus provid-
> ing a confusing and inelegant view of its shape. Our preference for
> Matthew Arnold's Hellenistic ideals risks obscuring the Hebraic side
> of our culture. The transformation of freedom into a moral concept
> and its pairing with duty is defalcated and tenuous in Locke. The dis-
> ciplinarian side of the American character is more readily attributed
> to our Puritan heritage.[16]

Understanding how these non-Greco-Roman traditions formed American
identity generally and Black identity specifically remains as relevant as ever.
With the elections of Barak Obama and Kamala Harris in the last fifteen

years, understanding aspects of the Black rhetorical tradition and its affin-
ity for the prophetic has particular political and democratic salience for our
nation. What John Ernest says about history remains relevant to rhetoric:
"We need to re-envision the theater of history so as to recognize the historical
authority of a wider range of performances, performances designed specifically to promote a liberating application of the past."[17] Prophetic rhetoric
and call narratives provide the first step in that reenvisioning process. They
seek specifically to call for a *remembrance* of the sacred and an imaginative
reflection on what the future *could be.*

PROPHECY CALLS FOR RETHINKING POLITICS, STATECRAFT, AND THE SECULAR-SACRED BINARY

Because the African American prophetic tradition has roots in the Hebrew
Bible and thus functions as a subset of religious rhetoric, Western scholars
still implicitly working with modernity's dichotomies may see it as contrary to the neo-Aristotelian emphasis on politics and statecraft. Below, I
discuss more fully the dismantling of these binaries, but for now, I merely
note that Black theology and prophecy, as evidenced in the call narratives
under consideration, do not rend religion from politics. The African American prophetic tradition's interest in politics rivals the neo-Aristotelian's;
however, it does take a decidedly different direction by focusing on moral
judgments and declining the delusion of detachment and objectivity. In
their call narratives, Maria Stewart and Nat Turner clearly understand the
categorically political consequences of their rhetoric and their disassem-
bling of secular-sacred binaries. These prophetic figures demand the deconstruction of modernity's binaries by revealing them as oppressive—not
mere implications of their rhetoric. Stewart, for example, articulates her
call narrative in response to the challenge of her being public as a Black
woman. She continues to ask, "What if I am a woman?" and argues for the
biblical, traditional, and social contributions of women in prophecy and
politics. Similarly, Turner subverts Thomas Gray's white political interests
and leverages his call narrative and the embodied rhetoric of martyrdom to
preserve the moral significance of Black freedom in the mind of white and
Black hearers. Thus, from the outset of their prophetic messaging, an aspect
of their thesis involves the expansion of the definition of political beyond
white male elite interests to include the resistance rhetoric and witness of
those on the margins.

PROPHECY PROVIDES INSIGHT INTO
IDEOGRAPHIC AND IDEOLOGICAL SUBVERSION

Like much postmodern and feminist discourse and criticism, the African American prophetic tradition, as exemplified in the call narratives discussed, has an interest in the liberative dismantling of ideology and critiques of the will to power. As the shells of ideology and power, ideographs provide unique opportunities for dismantling and demystifying ideological agendas, like white supremacy, patriarchy, and nationalism.

The unique contribution of prophetic rhetoric to ideograph and ideological subversion lies in the fact that prophetic rhetoric's primary opposition is idolatry. Whereas in the ancient world, an idol was a physical object representing a false claim about "ultimate reality" or the "ultimate truth" of the world, our contemporary conceptions of ultimate reality and truth are represented in our language-based ideologies. In a sense, then, from the prophet's perspective, a critique of the verbal symbols of ideology (ideographs) parallels the biblical prophets' critique of material symbols of idolatry (idols). Idols and ideologies get critiqued by prophetic figures not merely because they are *wrong* but because they are unjust and support systems of injustice. Prophets arise precisely to counter these false claims of ultimate reality and call instead for justice.[18]

Maria Stewart challenged gendered ideographs of the cult of true womanhood when she asked, "What if I am a woman?" while speaking about politics and religion in public. Throughout the speech and her call narrative, this question functions less as an interrogative and more like a direct statement. The form of the statement is stereotypically female: an interrogative with a direct use of a female pronoun. Yet she asks no real question. Instead, she makes a statement through the question: "I am a woman." Her direct assertion of her identity (not a role, like wife, mother, or servant) conjoins female content with a masculine structural shell. She thus intentionally subverts the male-female categories and ideographs (and their accompanying roles and rhetoric), confusing them and breaking down the implications of such binaries for Black women in the public sphere.

Also, Richard Allen employs the ideographs of *labor* and *gospel* throughout his autobiography. Allen combines these ideographs, which function in white Protestant circles as opposites, to provide a perspective by incongruity whereby the only true preachers of the gospel refuse to separate the body and work from the spirit and salvation. In this, Allen justifies the superiority of his own prophetic calling, his church plant, and his split from the larger white Methodist movement. Thus, both figures chose to become heretics to the dominant culture by intentionally misusing ideographs. They experienced and rhetorically thrived as exiles from the dominant political, religious, white masculine consciousness.

PROPHECY INVITES EXPLORATION OF UNSTUDIED RHETORS, PARTICULARLY BLACK WOMEN

To explore rhetorics outside the Greco-Roman traditions inherently entails the mining of rhetorical artifacts produced by figures outside the Greco-Roman traditions. Our collective cultural and disciplinary ignorance of such figures communicates how whiteness and patriarchy still dominate our discipline. Jacqueline Jones Royster and Gesa E. Kirsch have relevant comments:

> I marveled, in fact, at the number of times after a panel presentation of my research that I would receive a line of response like: How can what you're saying be true? African American women in the nineteenth century were slaves. They couldn't really read and write, could they? They didn't publish anything, did they? Where would they have done that? Where/How did you find any evidence for these sorts of claims? In other words, the lives, work, and contributions of women of African descent were functioning during that time within what I came to call an atmosphere of deep disbelief. Such questions suggested that as a group, African American women were perceived as a monolithic blob of humanity with inferior prospects and quite questionable value.[19]

Their experience verifies my own. Having presented at the National Communication Association on a few occasions, I have found myself as one of the few—and sometimes the *only*—white person in the room listening to papers on Black rhetoric. Sometimes I have been the only *male* in the room when delivering or listening to papers on Black women's rhetoric.

Prophetic rhetoric challenges our patriarchy and racism and calls us to reimagine rhetoric apart from the strictures of our white masculine traditions. Indeed, for white scholars, it calls on us to begin with presence and listening. What Schultze says about religiously sensitive scholarship applies, as well, to racially sensitive scholarship:

> Perhaps listening, not speaking, is the basis for religiously sensitive scholarship. . . . In the Hebrew and Christian tradition the idea of listening came out of the concept of "being obedient." To listen was to

risk personal and collective change by considering the wisdom from outside the self and tribe. Today academicians are paradigmatically tribal creatures who tend to listen only intra-collegially. This is why, in my view, the religious turn in postmodernism is so remarkable. By admitting the relative chaos in academe, postmodern scholars are challenging their own legitimation in society. Such listening could be scholars' own undoing or salvation—depending on how they frame the situation.[20]

We cannot understand American rhetoric, American radical rhetoric, or American feminist rhetoric without taking Black rhetoric into account. African American rhetors have challenged the very notions of America, masculinity, and femininity for centuries. At this moment, we have a unique opportunity to listen to and exalt their radical prophetic voices.

James Darsey began this discussion with prophetic rhetoric, but his failure to include the voices of people of color or women severely limited his scope, insights, and conclusions. Reading and studying prophetic rhetoric and call narratives help us reengage that discussion from the margins, which benefits a wider audience than the rhetorical communities we study. Listening to and exalting voices from the margins may also help us further develop theoretical models for understanding both oppressive rhetoric and rhetorics of resistance. As Woodyard notes, "If rhetorical scholars engage the project of building our theoretical understanding of prophecy to mirror the prophetic-liberating principle inherent in the Hebrew Bible, we will more fully come to terms with the 'exigencies of oppression' confronting not only women but every disaffected group or class."[21] Indeed, coming to terms with the exigencies of oppression naturally leads to realizing and investigating prophetic rhetoric's most counterintuitive assumption: some audiences are unpersuadable.

PROPHECY CALLS US TO INVESTIGATE THE UNDERSTANDING OF "FAILED" RHETORIC AND UNPERSUADABLE AUDIENCES

Neo-Aristotelian rhetorical traditions assume the primacy of persuasion or effect as the telos of oratory. As Lloyd F. Bitzer says, "A work of rhetoric is pragmatic; it comes into existence for the sake of something beyond itself; it functions ultimately to produce action or change in the world; it performs some task."[22] The pragmatism of this assumption has not gone unchallenged in communication studies. For example, Edwin Black argues that neo-Aristotelianism's pragmatic criticism is circular and too simplistic in its notions of causation. In the end, Black argues that neo-Aristotelianism ends up reaffirming the critic's perspective while never actually assessing the speech. For Black, effect is impossible to determine, and any certitude around it merely reflects the scholar's bias.[23] The results orientation dismisses prophetic rhetoric out of hand based on its inability or disinterest to produce effect.[24]

Figures in the African American prophetic tradition have long known with Charland that

> rhetorical theory's privileging of an audience's freedom to judge is problematic, for it assumes that audiences, with their prejudices, interests, and motives, are *given* and so extra-rhetorical. . . . [M]uch of what we as rhetorical critics consider to be a product or consequence of discourse, including social identity, religious faith, sexuality, and ideology is beyond the realm of rational or even free choice, beyond the realm of persuasion.[25]

The Hebrew prophet Isaiah said this very thing in his call narrative: "Seeing they will not see, hearing they will not hear."[26] Scholars from Aristotle through Wichelns have thought persuasion was the point of rhetoric;[27] Isaiah presumed persuasion was intermittently impossible.

Because prophetic rhetoric works with different expectations than Greco-Roman rhetoric, an evaluation must use alternative or adapted tools that can "illuminate, and provide some means for evaluating, the dynamic when prophecy fails."[28] My analysis of Nat Turner provides a unique opportunity to evaluate such rhetoric because Turner understands the imminence of his death during the interview with Thomas Gray. Indeed, Turner has chosen death as an aspect of a cruciform embodiment of prophetic discourse. For Turner, martyrdom is an embodied, reasonable, rhetorical response to audience intransigence.

Recognizing his audience's obstinacy, Turner embraces martyrdom *not* because he thinks verbal or moral rhetoric may convince his audience but because his objective before an unpersuadable audience is simply to witness, to preserve a morally significant event in the mind of the hearers. Martyrdom presupposes the audience's violent rejection of the prophet's message; thus, the prophet cannot find validation in immediate effect. If the message has any effect at all, it comes after the prophet's death. At best, the prophet's life, death, and calling produce an effect in a later audience.

With traditional neo-Aristotelian standards, prophetic rhetoric, messages of martyrdom, and engagement with intransigent audiences position prophetic rhetoric as a unique contributor to the field of rhetorical criticism by moving our discipline further away from the centrality of effect. Prophets understand beforehand that their audiences are not necessarily "free to be persuaded" because their prior moral commitments predate and are "logically prior" to persuasion.[29] Prophets understand that audiences are interpolated, fictively and rhetorically *created*, prior to and even after the rhetorical moment. Still, in the context of interpolation and intransigence, the prophet's duty lies in speaking "to the people, 'whether they hear or refuse to hear.'"[30]

In a contemporary setting, this explains Karlyn Kohrs Campbell's reflection on Elizabeth Cady Stanton's "tragic view" that "feminism cannot change the human condition."[31] Campbell recognizes the likely failure of persuasion, so feminist rhetoric tries to interpolate, mythologize, and renarrate the audience away from patriarchal ideology into narratives of liberation and justice. This renarration, however, requires audience buy-in that often goes against the material interests of men and, sometimes, the immediate material interests of the women. Thus, feminists recognize their audiences are not free subjects. Their history has determined and constrained their identity and imagination. The prophetic tradition calls this "sin" and describes it as an effective force of death and oppression, caging and shackling individual and collective *response* to messages of liberation. Sin gives power to patriarchy and interpolates its prisoners, thus minimizing the effect of the prophet's liberating rhetoric and agenda.

As it has come to us from the nineteenth century into the present, the African American prophetic tradition continues to wrestle with the lack of effect. Whether Dr. Martin Luther King's increasing pessimism toward the end of his life or the protest rhetoric of Black Lives Matter, Black prophetic rhetoric understands the minimal impact of their appeals even when utilizing ideographs white Americans find favorable (patriotism, freedom, etc.). All available means of persuasion have been utilized, yet prophecy and protest continue without a hearing. Thus, in their protest, prophets do not presume their protest can rationally persuade their opponents. They do not choose irrationality; they merely recognize the limited effect of rationality. Thus, their primary objective lies in witness. This is why Nat Turner "does not see his battle merely in the secular sense of a slave insurrection. . . . He continued to present his narrative in the metaphysics of a holy war."[32]

In the end, Kenneth Burke asks, "If a man takes great pains to obtain the approval of his group, does he not thereby give evidence that he needs to be approved?"[33] Burke implies an affirmative answer, but prophetic rhetoric points toward a negative one. Prophets enter rhetorical situations using identification *consciously* to ensure their witness is preserved no matter if it persuades. Thus, prophets exhibit a steadfast refusal to adapt to audience expectations. The audience's approval or applause remains irrelevant because, from the prophet's perspective, the audience's moral universe has shackled them into oppressive ideologies and idolatries (sin) that drive what they approve and applaud.

PROPHECY PROVIDES FURTHER INSIGHT INTO RESISTANCE RHETORIC

Much value lies in studying the rhetoric of oppressors, as Burke says, so we can understand what kind of medicine these medicine men "concocted, that we may know, with greater accuracy, exactly what to guard against, if we are to forestall the concocting of similar medicine."[34] However, scholars who study the various sites of oppression (gender, race, class, etc.) have also noted the value of studying resistance rhetoric, the meaning-making mechanisms of those who resist oppression. In America, the resistance rhetoric of the Black, Afrocentric, and African American prophetic tradition deserves further analysis: "In the context of historical and current oppression, African rhetoric is also a rhetoric of resistance. Clearly, given a community forcibly transferred to America during the holocaust of enslavement and systematically oppressed since then, a central aspect of the corpus of African American rhetorical practice is rooted in and reflective of constant resistance."[35]

By studying resistance rhetoric across disciplines, we may observe that oppression's intersectionality may find opposition in the intersectionality of resistance rhetoric and tactics. In various resistance rhetorics, including prophetic rhetoric, we see an intentional refusal of respectability, a resolute rejection of audience expectation, a criticism of civility, and a disavowal of decorum. In other words, a study of prophetic rhetoric may exchange insights with other resistance rhetorics. After all, all "resistance is necessarily a response to, and in its varied expressions partly determined by, the varied manifestations of power. The realm of the imaginary, the visionary, the utopic is discovered and cultivated by those who define themselves as pressed and limited in some significant ways by power, as a means of resisting such power."[36]

PROPHECY CHALLENGES MODERNITY'S ARTIFICIAL BINARIES

One reason the study of prophetic rhetoric challenges the discipline of communication and rhetoric lies in its rejection of modernity's binaries, which are still lively and operative in our discipline. Indeed, prophetic rhetoric highlights that such binaries not only are foreign to our figures but also function in the context of a colonial agenda designed to solidify the hegemony of white men. Reggie L. Williams discusses the social implications of *splitting* theology and religion into false binaries:

> The project of theology in colonialism was split in this assembly; it was primarily doctrinal and conceptual, lacking content for Christian conduct. That split was necessary to justify the domination of foreign human bodies that accompanied classifying human beings by race, securing the advantages of whiteness, and accommodating the practices of colonialism. . . . Colonial Christianity engineered a modified theology that was bred to resist empathy and the practice of incarnation.[37]

Given the colonialist, racist, and patriarchal breeding of these binaries and our figures' rejection of such, we must rethink them.

Admittedly, many figures from the African American prophetic tradition, even Maria Stewart and Richard Allen, operated to a degree with Enlightenment assumptions. Still, these assumptions were not wholesale adopted. Stephen G. Hall notes the complicated nature of nineteenth-century Black participation in Enlightenment thinking: "Although they usually rejected the tendency common among Enlightenment theorists to divide the world into a classic binary—the civilized and the savage—these [nineteenth-century Black] intellectuals were strong proponents of the Enlightenment vision of the world suffused with reason."[38] Reason, keep in mind, does not contrast with religion. Rather, religion provides the foundation for reason. Reason evidences a rational creator.

The African American prophetic tradition's refusal to bifurcate religion and reason mirrors the Hebrew prophets' refusal to bifurcate the spiritual and material worlds. As Gerhard von Rad notes, prophets make

> no distinction between spiritual and material—the two are intertwined in the closest possible way; and in consequence he is also unable properly to differentiate between word and object, idea and actuality. Such thought is thus characterized by an inherent absence of differentiation between the ideal and the real, or between word and object; these coalesce as if both stood on the plane of being. . . . Thus, in a very realistic sense, what happens in language is that the world is given material expression.[39]

In the prophet's biblical interpretive lens, the cosmos exists because words and reality, religion and reason, spiritual and material, and secular and sacred exist together. This holistic, harmonious view of the world calls into question modernity's binaries and creates the conditions for justice. This explains why abolitionist and civil rights activists seamlessly employ the language of religion and rights, secularity and sacrality.[40]

The rejection of modernity's binaries aligns with the resistance efforts and civil rights efforts of feminist rhetorical scholarship. Royster and Kirsch comment, "Our move is also to disrupt the public-private divide by suggesting a more fully textured sense of what it means to place these women in social space, rather than private space or public space."[41] Black freedom and women's liberation are concurrently personal, political, and intersectionally correlated:[42] "In the ongoing evolution of resistance and struggle . . . we join those who want to recognize, not only the artificiality of public-private dichotomies as demonstrated, for example, through feminist analyses of public and private spheres, but also to recognize that dualities (two-ness, double-consciousness, margin-center relationships) are more often than not multiplicities."[43] For Royster and Kirsch, a metaphor of concentric circles of social relationships, cross-generational connections, and geographic distances explain the rhetoric of women and racial minorities far better than "a less-productive view that attempts to track boundaries between public and private domains."[44] Tamura Lomax uses stronger language when addressing the oppressiveness of binaries in sexual rhetoric: "A sexual discourse of resistance compels us to rethink cultural texts and notions that divide the black body and black soul, misread black sexuality as a thing to exploit, and encourage black sexual shame and secrecy."[45] Thus, intersectional oppression operates linguistically and socially via the openly hidden confines of conceptual binaries constructed to bolster white male hegemony. Prophetic rhetoric and resistance rhetorics help "us see beyond one of our most-basic underinterrogated assumptions, the concept of 'woman/female-man/male' and helps us to notice new terrains for exploration, documentation, analysis, and interpretation that push us to a more richly rendered view of rhetoric as a diversely articulated human enterprise."[46]

Instead of a binary-riddled rhetoric, the African American prophetic tradition joins with the resistance rhetoric of feminism and Afrocentricity to propose a hermeneutic and rhetoric of harmony. Understanding that figures in the prophetic tradition use biblical texts, scholars can help alleviate oppressive uses of the Bible not through a hermeneutic of suspicion but through a hermeneutic of harmony by proposing thoughtful interpretations of the Bible that create liberation and harmony in the world. Such an effort aligns with the liberative hermeneutics within the African American prophetic tradition and Afrocentric rhetoric because, as noted, "within African cultures, the greatest power on earth is the ability to create harmony in place of disharmony, order where once where there was chaos."[47] As in the Bible, harmony is created through speech acts where the oppressed community seeks common cause.[48]

Scholars need not even share the prophetic figures' religious worldview, but the common cause can heal the wounds of modernity's binaries. As Royster and Kirsch conclude, "Even if and when we find ourselves disagreeing in the end with their values, ideologies, or beliefs, we will still look and listen carefully and caringly, contemplate our perceptions, and speculate about the promise, potential, and realities of these rhetors' lives and work."[49] Such deconstruction, however, requires moral courage on the part of critics.

PROPHECY CALLS US TO CRITICAL, MORAL COURAGE

Committing to honesty in a white academy and church, which have historical and material interests dedicated in some ways to *misinterpreting* the world, takes moral courage. When I first entered the communication department at the University of Memphis, I had never heard of Quintilian, but I wanted to become something like his "good man speaking well,"[50] a person who could articulate justice and goodness in a world of injustice. This commitment shaped my scholarship and led me to seek models who engage texts and criticism with moral courage.

Edwin Black, among others, models the power of such moral commitments when he challenges communication critics to consider that the problem with the Coatesville address may not lie within the speech or the orator but within the white audience's prior (im)moral commitments. These (im)moral commitments to white supremacy led John Jay Chapman's audience to *misinterpret* lynching as just and good. Black, then, notes that the speaker, the text, and the audience all intermingle in a myriad of morally complex ways:

> Our perceptions of this event will be colored by our moral dispositions. Hence, there would conceivably be those who would perceive it as a hideous expression of mob violence; there would be those who would perceive it, clinically, as the concrete illustration of an abstract sociopathic idea; there would be those who would refuse to perceive the event at all, who would dismiss it and put it out of mind.[51]

Black explains that the intransigence of an audience may indicate prior moral commitments, not necessarily stylistic shortcomings. His essay calls on critics to consider the moral consequences of a discourse. Herein, he laid the groundwork for future scholars to further explore the connection between moral commitments and academic criticism. James F. Klumpp and Thomas A. Hollihan, for example, take up Black's call when they argue, "There is a task for the rhetoric critic that goes beyond interest in 'mere' rhetoric. The critic that emerges—the interpreter, the teacher, the social actor—is a moral participant, cognizant of the power and responsibility that accompanies full critical participation in his/her society."[52]

Molefi Kete Asante's Afrocentric rhetorical criticism also prioritizes ethics:

> The aim of good criticism is to pass judgment, and judgment is concerned with good and bad, right and wrong; criticism is, therefore, preeminently an ethical act. . . . The Afrocentric critic is also concerned with ethical judgments but finds the aesthetic judgment equally valuable, particularly as the substantial ground upon which to make a decision about the restoration of harmony and balance. Indeed, Afrocentric criticism essentially combines ethics and aesthetics.[53]

For Asante, good criticism asks whether the orator contributed to the moral harmony between people and people, people and the divine, or people and themselves.

As a white critic, my goals of hearing, highlighting, citing, and learning from the marginalized voices in this book spring from a desire to deepen my moral commitment to justice. I desire not only the critical skills to interpret the events described in the Coatesville address but to be the kind of critic and person who can interpret them with moral courage. Moral courage does not merely necessitate academic aptitude but insists on adherence to moral commitments. Moral commitments lead naturally to prophetic rhetoric, which both makes ethical appeals and knows beforehand that some audiences are not necessarily "free to be persuaded" because their moral commitments are "logically prior" to persuasion."[54] Prophetic rhetoric takes seriously the need for moral courage from the speaker, the audience, the text, and, yes, even the critic. For in the end, such perilous persuasive efforts may indeed leave us isolated from our fellow humans, especially those with power and privilege—those to whom prophecy calls out.

$\mathcal{N}otes$

PREFACE

1. David A. Frank, "Arguing with God, Talmudic Discourse, and the Jewish Countermodel: Implications for the Study of Argumentation," *Argumentation and Advocacy* 41 (Fall 2004): 73.

2. Gen. 1:1, 1:5 (two times), 1:6, 1:8, 1:9, 1:10, 1:11, 1:20, 1:22, 1:24, 1:26, 1:28, 1:29, and 2:3.

3. Gen. 1:26–28.

4. This theme of rule through rhetoric comes up again in the second creation story when the man (Adam) *names* all the animals of creation as an indicator of his rule over them. Gen. 2:19–20.

5. Kenneth Burke, *Language as Symbolic Action: Essays On Life, Literature and Method* (Berkeley: University of California, 1968), 16.

6. Abraham J. Heschel, *Who Is Man?* (Stanford: Stanford University Press, 1965), 5. Of course, some contend that in the Hebrew Bible tradition, there is no distinction between symbol and reality. Frank, "Arguing with God," 73.

7. "There is abundant evidence that other cosmologies existed in Israel. Scattered illusions to be found in the prophetic, poetic, and wisdom literature of the Bible testify to a popular belief that prior to the onset of the creative process the powers of watery chaos had to be subdued by God. These mythical beings are variously designated Yam (Sea), Nahar (River), Leviathan (Coiled One), Rahab (Arrogant One), and Tannin (Dragon)." Nahum Sarna, *Genesis: The JPS Torah Commentary* (Philadelphia, PA: Jewish Publication Society, 1989), 3.

8. Walter Brueggemann, *Genesis: Interpretation* (Louisville, KY: John Knox Press, 1982), 25.

9. In the Enuma Elish, the Babylonian creation myth, creation results from a war for power between gods of the Babylonian pantheon. John H. Walton, *The Lost World of Genesis One* (Downers Grove: InterVarsity Press, 2009), 28.

10. Ronald L. Jackson, "Afrocentricity as Metatheory: A Dialogic Exploration of Its Principles," in *Understanding African American Rhetoric: Classical Origins to Contemporary Innovations*, ed. Ronald L. Jackson and Elain B. Johnson (New York: Routledge, 2003), 121.

11. This element of Genesis 1 aligns with Sonja K. Foss and Cindy L. Griffin's notion of *invitational rhetoric*. "Although we believe persuasion is often necessary, we believe an

128 Notes

alternative exists that may be used in instances when changing and controlling of others is not the rhetor's goal." Sonja K. Foss and Cindy L. Griffin, "Beyond Persuasion: A Proposal for Invitational Rhetoric," in *Contemporary Rhetorical Theory: A Reader*, 2nd ed., ed. Mark J. Porrovecchio and Celeste Michelle Condit (New York: Guilford Press, 2016), 79.

12. Brueggemann, *Genesis*, 14.

13. Abraham J. Heschel, *The Insecurity of Freedom: Essays on Human Existence* (New York: Schocken, 1972), 13.

14. "Creation is what it is because God commands it. But the command is not authoritarian. It is, rather, 'let there be.'" Brueggemann, *Genesis*, 30. This inviting command inherently refuses violence, a refusal to resort to pure force.

15. Brueggemann, *Genesis*, 25.

16. Abraham J. Heschel, *The Prophets* (New York: HarperCollins, 1962), 277.

17. Molefi Kete Asante, "Maat and Human Communication: Supporting Identity, Culture, and History without Global Domination," *Intercultural Communication Studies* 20, no. 1 (2011): 52.

18. James Darsey states,

When the events of history reach inhuman and incomprehensible proportions, theories of human culpability are no longer adequate. New Causes commensurate with the terror of the perceived effects must be sought. In the history of the ancient Jews, this time was the end of the sixth century B.C.E., the time of the Babylonian Exile. The Exile was a crisis of unmatched intensity, involving as it did the burning of Jerusalem, the surrender of self-government for the Jewish people, and the end of the Davidic succession. Constrained to work within the here and now of events, prophetic theology demanded that Yahweh reveal Himself in this world through a correspondence between causes and effects. At the time of the Exile, the guilt required to account for events was unbearable, opening Yahweh's control of history to question.

James Darsey, *The Prophetic Tradition and Radical Rhetoric in America* (New York: New York University Press, 1997), 116.

19. Raymie E. McKerrow, "Critical Rhetoric: Theory and Praxis," in *Readings in Rhetorical Criticism*, 5th ed., ed. Carl R. Burgchardt and Hillary A. Jones (State College: Strata, 2017), 82–83.

20. McKerrow, "Critical Rhetoric," 88.

21. Walter R. Fisher, "Narration as Human Communication Paradigm: The Case of Public Moral Argument," *Communication Monographs* 51, no. 1 (1984): 1–22.

A PERILOUS INTRODUCTION

1. Jarena Lee, "The Life and Religious Experience of Jarena Lee, a Coloured Lady: Giving Account of Her Call to Preach the Gospel," in *Sisters of the Spirit: Three Black Women's Autobiographies of the Nineteenth Century*, ed. William L. Andrews (Bloomington: Indiana University Press, 1986), 44.

2. Walter Brueggemann, *The Prophetic Imagination*, 2nd ed. (Minneapolis, MN: Fortress Press, 2001).

3. Darsey, *Prophetic Tradition*, 16.

4. Darsey, *Prophetic Tradition*, 16.

5. Darsey, *Prophetic Tradition*, 21.

6. Kerith M. Woodyard, "'If by Martyrdom I Can Advance My Race One Step, I Am Ready for It': Prophetic *Ethos* and the Reception of Elizabeth Cady Stanton's *The Woman's Bible*," *Journal of Communication and Religion* 31, no. 2 (November 2008): 276.

7. Kerith M. Woodyard, "Depatriarchalizing in Rhetorical Theory: Toward a Feminist Prophetic Tradition," *Ohio Communication Journal* 48 (October 2010): 32.

8. Woodyard, "Martyrdom," 275.

9. Woodyard, "Martyrdom," 280. Emphasis original.

10. Woodyard, "Depatriarchalizing in Rhetorical Theory," 29.

11. Darsey, *Prophetic Tradition*, 206.

12. Andre E. Johnson, *The Forgotten Prophet: Bishop Henry McNeal Turner and the African American Prophetic Tradition* (Lanham, MD: Lexington Books, 2012), 4.

13. Elie Wiesel, *Night*, rev. ed., trans. Marion Wiesel (New York: Hill and Wang, 2006), vii.

14. Wiesel, *Night*, viii.

15. Wiesel, *Night*, ix.

16. A. Johnson, *Forgotten Prophet*, 10.

17. A. Johnson, *Forgotten Prophet*, 7.

18. A. Johnson, *Forgotten Prophet*, 14.

19. Gerhard von Rad, *The Message of the Prophets* (New York: Harper and Row, 1965), 84.

20. Christopher Z. Hobson, *The Mount of Vision: African American Prophetic Tradition, 1800–1950* (Oxford: Oxford University Press, 2012), xiii.

21. Hobson, *Mount of Vision*, 37–39.

22. Hobson, *Mount of Vision*, 39–40.

23. I say "primary" because the Black congregation may also need to do their own turning. However, Black turning is not only socially secondary but also ethically secondary—that is, the Black auditor needs to turn only insofar as they have assumed the superiority of whiteness or adopted, even if unwittingly, the assumptions of or behaviors that contribute to white supremacy.

24. Hobson, *Mount of Vision*, 40–41.

25. Hobson, *Mount of Vision*, 41–42.

26. Jeremiah Wright, "(2003) Rev. Jeremiah Wright, 'Confusing God and Government,'" BlackPast, May 6, 2008, https://www.blackpast.org/african-american-history/2008-rev-jeremiah-wright-confusing-god-and-government/.

27. Kenneth Burke, *Permanence and Change: An Anatomy of Purpose* (Berkeley: University of California Press, 1984), 74.

28. Sometimes prophets do not even want to persuade, as in the case of the eighth-century BCE prophet Jonah, who expressed suicidal regret when his minimalist rhetoric succeeded. "Forty days more, and Nineveh shall be overthrown." Jon. 3:4 (NRSV).

29. Claus Westermann, *Basic Forms of Prophetic Speech*, trans. Hugh Clayton White (Louisville, KY: Westminster / John Knox Press, 1991), 26.

30. Karlyn Kohrs Campbell and Kathleen Hall Jamieson, "Form and Genre in Rhetorical Criticism: An Introduction," in *Form and Genre: Shaping Rhetorical Action*, ed. Karlyn Kohrs Campbell and Kathleen Hall Jamieson (Falls Church: Speech Communication Association, 1976), 15.

31. Hugh Dalziel Duncan, introduction to *Permanence and Change: An Anatomy of Purpose*, by Kenneth Burke (Berkeley: University of California Press, 1984), xxv.

32. Hobson, *Mount of Vision*, 11.

33. Karlyn Kohrs Campbell, "The Rhetoric of Women's Liberation: An Oxymoron," *Quarterly Journal of Speech* 59, no. 1 (February 1973): 78.

34. Von Rad, *Message of the Prophets*, 37.

35. Campbell and Jamieson, "Form and Genre," 5.

36. Von Rad, *Message of the Prophets*, 18.

37. Campbell and Jamieson, "Form and Genre," 422.

38. Carolyn R. Miller, "Genre as Social Action," *Quarterly Journal of Speech* 70, no. 2 (1984): 151.

39. Von Rad, *Message of the Prophets*, 78.

40. Von Rad, *Message of the Prophets*, 80.

41. Von Rad, *Message of the Prophets*, 81–82.

42. Isa. 1:12–15 (NRSV).

43. Von Rad, *Message of the Prophets*, 93.

44. Heschel, *Prophets*, xxvii.

45. Von Rad, *Message of the Prophets*, 10–11.

46. Hobson, *Mount of Vision*, 90.

47. Molefi Kete Asante, *The Afrocentric Idea* (Philadelphia, PA: Temple University Press, 1998), 34.

48. Rodney H. Jones, *Discourse Analysis: A Resources Book for Students*, 2nd. ed. (New York: Routledge, 2019), 9.

49. Richard T. Hughes, *Myths America Lives By: White Supremacy and the Stories That Give Us Meaning* (Urbana: University of Illinois Press, 2018).

50. Alan D. DeSantis, "An Amostic Prophecy: Frederick Douglass' *The Meaning of the Fourth of July for the Negro*," *Journal of Communication and Religion* 22, no. 1 (1999): 76.

51. Frederick Douglass, "What to the Slave Is the Fourth of July?," July 5, 1892, Teaching American History, accessed April 16, 2024, https://teachingamericanhistory.org/library/document/what-to-the-slave-is-the-fourth-of-july/.

52. DeSantis, "Amostic Prophecy," 66.

53. Douglass, "What to the Slave."

54. Douglass, "What to the Slave."

55. Michael Calvin McGee, "The 'Ideograph': A Link between Rhetoric and Ideology," in *Readings in Rhetorical Criticism*, 5th ed., ed. Carl R. Burgchardt and Hillary A. Jones (State College: Strata, 2017), 476.

56. McGee, "Ideograph," 476.

57. McGee, "Ideograph," 468.

58. Heschel, *Prophets*, 252.

59. Kenneth Burke, *A Rhetoric of Motives* (Berkeley: University of California Press, 1969), 79.

60. Jacqueline Jones Royster and Gesa E. Kirsch, *Feminist Rhetorical Practices: New Horizons for Rhetoric, Composition, and Literacy Studies* (Carbondale: Southern Illinois University Press, 2012), chap. 5, loc. 997 of 2384, Kindle.

61. Brueggemann, *Prophetic Imagination*, 3.

62. Andre E. Johnson, "'To Make the World So Damn Uncomfortable': W. E. B. Du Bois and the African American Prophetic Tradition," *Carolinas Communication Annual* 32 (2016): 19.

63. Robert Alter, *The Hebrew Bible: A Translation with Commentary*, vol. 2, *Prophets* (New York: W. W. Norton, 2019), xlvii–xlviii.

64. Brueggemann, *Prophetic Imagination*, 4.

65. Brueggemann, *Prophetic Imagination*, 18.

66. James H. Cone, *Speaking the Truth: Ecumenism, Liberation, and Black Theology* (Grand Rapids, MI: Eerdmans, 1986), 16.

67. Nancy Duarte, *Resonate: Present Visual Stories That Transform Audiences* (Hoboken, NJ: John Wiley and Sons, 2010), 206.

68. Von Rad, *Message of the Prophets*, 12.

69. Von Rad, *Message of the Prophets*, 12.

70. Wilda C. Gafney, *Daughters of Miriam: Women Prophets in Ancient Israel* (Minneapolis, MN: Fortress Press, 2008), 23.

71. Edwin Black, "The Second Persona," in *Contemporary Rhetorical Theory: A Reader*, 2nd ed., ed. Mark J. Porrovecchio and Celeste Michelle Condit (New York: Guilford Press, 2016), 296.

72. Andre E. Johnson, "The Prophetic Persona of James Cone and the Rhetorical Theology of Black Theology," *Black Theology: An International Journal* 8, no. 3 (2010): 268.

73. Hobson, *Mount of Vision*, 155.

74. A. Johnson, "Prophetic Persona," 268.

75. My definition here resembles that of Andre E. Johnson's. I merely add to Johnson's definition the concepts of generically multiformal, ideograph-subverting, and later communal affirmation—none of which are foreign to his analysis. A. Johnson, "To Make the World," 18.

76. W. E. B. Du Bois, *The Souls of Black Folk* (New York: Cosimo Classics, 2007).

77. Woodyard, "Depatriarchalizing in Rhetorical Theory," 30.

78. Kristen Lynn Majocha rightly notes, "The literature on prophetic rhetoric overlaps genres, including religion, theology, communication studies, and religious communication studies, as well as other fields of academic inquiry." Kirsten Lynn Majocha, "Prophetic Rhetoric: A Gap between the Field of Study and the Real World," *Journal of Communication and Religion* 39, no. 4 (Winter 2016): 6.

CHAPTER 1. THE CALL NARRATIVE OF MARIA STEWART

1. This excerpt from the speech is reprinted from Maria W. Stewart, "What If I Am a Woman?," in *Lift Every Voice: African American Oratory, 1787–1900*, ed. Philip S. Foner and Robert James Branham (Tuscaloosa: University of Alabama Press, 1998), 135. Omission and other idiosyncrasies original.

2. Mark 5:7. Translation by author.

3. Stewart, "I Am a Woman," 137.

4. Kristin Waters, *Maria W. Stewart and the Roots of Black Political Thought* (Jackson: University Press of Mississippi, 2022), 227.

5. Mary P. Ryan, *Women in Public: Between Banner and Ballots, 1825–1880* (Baltimore, MD: John Hopkins University Press, 1990), 4.

6. "Institutionalized practices restricting access to resources are particularly effective in undercutting the growth and flourishing of young people, especially girls. . . . Stewart's keen awareness of the degree to which the twin-oppressors of excessive labor and thwarted education successfully enforce barriers to race, class, and gender excellence." Waters, *Maria W. Stewart*, 228–29.

7. Marilyn Richardson, *Maria Stewart: America's First Black Political Writer* (Bloomington: Indiana University Press, 1987), 30.

8. Rhana A. Gittens, "'What If I Am a Woman?': Black Feminist Rhetorical Strategies of Intersectional Identification and Resistance in Maria Stewart's Texts," *Southern Communication Journal* 83, no. 5 (2018): 311.

9. Stephen G. Hall, *A Faithful Account of the Race: African American Historical Writing in the Nineteenth Century* (Chapel Hill: University of North Carolina Press, 2009), 5.

10. Valerie C. Cooper, *Word, like Fire: Maria Stewart, the Bible, and the Rights of African Americans* (Charlottesville: University of Virginia Press, 2011), 4.

11. Shirley Wilson Logan, *"We Are Coming": The Persuasive Discourse of Nineteenth-Century Black Women* (Carbondale: Southern Illinois University Press, 1999), 33.

12. Nikki M. Taylor, *Driven toward Madness: The Fugitive Slave Margaret Garner and Tragedy on the Ohio* (Athens: Ohio University Press, 2016), 114–15.

13. Stewart, "I Am a Woman," 135. Stewart wrote this speech as she intended to leave Boston for New York, possibly to pursue more involvement with the abolitionist movement.

14. Waters, *Maria W. Stewart*, 241.

15. Waters, *Maria W. Stewart*, 241.

16. Cooper, *Word, like Fire*, 141.

17. Waters, *Maria W. Stewart*, 241.

18. Fisher, "Narration as Human Communication," 263.

19. Fisher, "Narration as Human Communication," 263.

20. Fisher, "Narration as Human Communication," 271.

21. Thomas Hoyt Jr., "Interpreting Biblical Scholarship for the Black Church Tradition," in *The Stony Road We Trod*, ed. Cain Hope Felder (Minneapolis, MN: Fortress Press, 1991), 25.

22. William H. Myers, *God's Yes Was Louder Than My No: Rethinking the African American Call to Ministry* (Eugene, OR: Wipf and Stock, 1994), 69.

23. Lee, "Life and Religious Experience."

24. Kimberly P. Johnson, "'Must Thee Take the Man Exclusively': Jarena Lee and Claiming the Right to Preach," *Listening: Journal of Communication Ethics, Religion, and Culture* 55, no. 3 (Fall 2020): 184.

25. Lee, "Life and Religious Experience," 44–45, quoted in K. Johnson, "Take the Man," 184.

26. K. Johnson, "Take the Man," 185.

27. Hobson, *The Mount of Vision*, 8.

28. Kevin Pelletier, *Apocalyptic Sentimentalism* (Athens: University of Georgia Press, 2015), 65.

29. Beth Allison Barr, *The Making of Biblical Womanhood: How the Subjugation of Women Became Gospel Truth* (Grand Rapids, MI: Brazos Press, 2021), 161–64.

30. Barr, *Making of Biblical Womanhood*, 155–56.

31. Cooper, *Word, like Fire*, 116.

32. Barr, *Making of Biblical Womanhood*, 156.

33. Phyllis M. Japp, "Esther or Isaiah? The Abolitionist-Feminist Rhetoric of Angelina Grimke," *Quarterly Journal of Speech* 71, no. 3 (1985): 337.

34. Japp, "Esther or Isaiah?," 342.

35. Cooper, *Word, like Fire*, 116.

36. Jamie L. Carlacio, "Speaking with and to Me: Discursive Positioning and the Unstable Categories of Race, Class, and Gender," in *Calling Cards: Theory and Practice in the Study of Race, Gender, and Culture*, ed. Jacqueline Jones Royster and Ann Marie Mann Simpkins (Albany: State University of New York Press, 2005), chap. 8, loc. 1603 of 3818, Kindle.

37. Carlacio, "Speaking," chap. 8, loc. 1610 of 3818.

38. Eddie S. Glaude Jr., *Exodus! Religion, Race, and Nation in Early Nineteenth-Century Black America* (Chicago: University of Chicago Press, 2000), 121.

39. Darsey, *Prophetic Tradition*, 16.

40. Darsey, *Prophetic Tradition*, 93.

41. We get hints of Maria W. Stewart wrestling with these assumptions, which she shares with her audiences: "I have thought thus publicly to express my sentiments before you. I hope my friends will not scrutinize these pages with too severe an eye, as I have not calculated to display either elegance or taste in their composition, but have merely written the meditations of my heart as far as my imagination led." Maria W. Stewart, *The Productions of Mrs. Maria W. Stewart Presented to the First Africa Baptist Church and Society, of the City of Boston* (Boston, MA: Friends of Freedom and Virtue, 1835), 2.

42. Von Rad, *Message of the Prophets*, 34.

43. Campbell, "Rhetoric of Women's Liberation," 78.

44. Campbell and Jamieson, "Form and Genre," 20.

45. Cooper, *Word, like Fire*, 18.

46. Summary provided in Hava Shalom-Guy, "The Call Narratives of Gideon and Moses: Literary Convention or More?," *Journal of the Hebrew Scriptures* 11 (2011): 3–4, https://doi.org/10.5508/jhs.2011.v11.a11. This structure finds affirmation in Daniel I. Block's discussion of the Hebrew prophet's call narratives, which he says, typically consist of "(1) a confrontation with God and/or his messenger; (2) an introductory address of the person being called; (3) the divine commission; (4) the raising of objections by the person called; (5) divine words of reassurance; and (6) a sign authenticating the call experience." Daniel I. Block, *Judges, Ruth*, New American Commentary 6 (Nashville, TN: Broadman and Holman, 1999), 257.

47. A. Johnson, "Prophetic Persona," 268.

48. Nicole McDonald shows how Julia Foote also plays with this rhetorical structure via (1) preparation—that is, God-ordained opportunities to exercise the gifts of proclamation before receiving the divine commission, with the purpose to gain familiarity with the

call; (2) divine commission—the command from God for a specific work, which identifies one's function in ministry; (3) resistance—the objection to God's call based on presumed insufficiency to fulfill the call; (4) affirmation of the call—the God-given sign directed to the chosen individual that confirms the call; (5) prayer—communication with God throughout the narrative; (6) supportive sisterhood, providing communal affirmation; and (7) acceptance—that is, when submission to the call occurs. Nicole McDonald, "From Resistance to Receiving: A Rhetorical Analysis of the Call Narrative of Julia A. J. Foote," *Listening: Journal of Communication, Ethics, Religion, and Culture* 55, no. 3 (Fall 2020): 223.

49. Maria W. Stewart, "Why Sit Ye Here and Die?," in *Lift Every Voice: African American Oratory, 1787–1900*, ed. Philip S. Foner and Robert James Branham (Tuscaloosa: University of Alabama Press, 1998), 127; Stewart, "I Am a Woman," 137.

50. Andre E. Johnson, "Introduction," *Listening: Journal of Communication, Ethics, Religion, and Culture* 55, no. 3 (Fall 2020): 148.

51. Pelletier, *Apocalyptic Sentimentalism*, 63.

52. Norm Habel, "The Form and Significance of the Call Narratives," *Zeitschrift für die alttestamentliche Wissenschaft* 77, no. 3 (1965): 297–323.

53. Eph. 4:14, wherein the apostle Paul calls the Ephesian church out of childlike thinking to the maturity of correct doctrine. Note added by author.

54. Stewart, "I Am a Woman," 139.

55. Mark 5:15, wherein the Gadarene demoniac—a *gentile, who is therefore without the promises of Israel*—is exercised and moves from irrational, demonic behavior to lucid, disciple-like behavior. This narrative is in contrast to the rejection of Israel as a whole (this gentile understands who Jesus is, while Israel misses it) and to the misunderstanding of Jesus's very own disciples throughout the entire Gospel of Mark. Note added by author.

56. Stewart, "I Am a Woman," 139. Emphasis added.

57. Pelletier, *Apocalyptic Sentimentalism*, 64.

58. Isa. 6:8 (NRSV).

59. Isa. 6:1 (NRSV).

60. Habel, "Form and Significance."

61. Hobson, *Mount of Vision*, 155.

62. Ezek. 36:15 (AV).

63. Willie Harrel Jr., "A Call to Political and Social Activism: The Jeremiadic Discourse of Maria Miller Stewart, 1831–1833," *Journal of International Women's Studies* 9, no. 3 (May 2008): 300–319.

64. Pelletier, *Apocalyptic Sentimentalism*, 66.

65. McKerrow, "Critical Rhetoric," 83.

66. McKerrow, "Critical Rhetoric," 84.

67. See, respectively, Jer. 1:6 (AV); Exod. 3:11 (AV).

68. Myers, *God's Yes*, 38.

69. Logan, *We Are Coming*, 36.

70. Matt. 26:39 (AV).

71. Matt. 20:20–28 (AV).

72. See Matt. 20:25–28.

73. Luke 22:42.

74. Stewart, "Why Sit Ye Here," 127.

75. Matt. 20:20–28 (AV).

76. Glaude, *Exodus!*, 122.

77. Stewart, "I Am a Woman," 139.

78. Stewart, "I Am a Woman," 137.

79. Stewart, "I Am a Woman," 137.

80. The rod she references could refer to the rod of the protective shepherd, who ensures the psalmist lacks nothing (Ps. 23:4). Or it could be the rod of discipline, with which a parent (in this case, God) disciplines a child (here, Stewart) for the purposes of obedience (Prov. 13:24). Or finally, it could reference Ps. 2, where both rods and kissing combine in a messianic litany that suggests the destruction of the Messiah's enemies—a prophetic warning to the kings of the nations and a call for all nations to kiss God's son/king lest he be angry. Any of these may make sense in Stewart's context.

81. Matt. 6:24.

82. Stewart, "I Am a Woman," 137.

83. Myers, *God's Yes*, 189.

84. Stewart, "I Am a Woman," 137.

85. Monika R. Alston-Miller, "The Influence of the Pauline Epistles on Maria W. Stewart's Rhetoric: A Political Gospel," *Journal of Communication and Religion* 38, no. 2 (Summer 2015): 100.

86. Stewart, "I Am a Woman," 137.

87. Stewart, "I Am a Woman," 137.

88. Stewart, "I Am a Woman," 137.

89. Stewart, "I Am a Woman," 138.

90. Myers, *God's Yes*, 62.

91. Stewart, "I Am a Woman," 137. Here, she is citing the Pauline text Rom. 15:29.

92. Stewart, "I Am a Woman," 137.

93. Stewart, "I Am a Woman," 138. Here, she cites Luke 1:64, which depicts the praise of Zachariah at the birth of his son, John the Baptist.

94. John 16:8; Deut. 18:18; Isa. 59:21; Jer. 1:9, 5:14; Ps. 35:4; Rev. 9:4.

95. Stewart, "I Am a Woman," 138.

96. Stewart, "I Am a Woman," 138.

97. Cooper, *Word, like Fire*, 149.

98. Darsey, *Prophetic Tradition*, 86. Emphasis original.

99. Myers, *God's Yes*, 115.

100. I elsewhere point this out as regards Martin Luther King Jr.'s prophetic-call narrative with his reference to midnight: "Whereas in *Stride Toward Freedom* King merely mentions that the event took place 'late, after a strenuous day,' the sermon adds scriptural significance through a shift in description. By pinpointing the precise and portentous nature of the time (midnight) when 'strange experiences' occur, King signals to his audience an Abraham-like experience of God." Thomas M. Fuerst, "A King's Place Is in the Kitchen: The Rhetorical Trajectory of the Rev. Dr. Martin Luther King, Jr.'s Kitchen Table Experience," *Listening: Journal of Communication, Ethics, Religion, and Culture* 55, no. 3 (Fall 2020): 164.

101. Royster and Kirsch, *Feminist Rhetorical Practices*, loc. 1370 of 2384.

CHAPTER 2. THE CALL NARRATIVE OF RICHARD ALLEN

1. Richard Allen, *The Life, Experience, and Gospel Labours of the Rt. Rev. Richard Allen* (Philadelphia, PA: Martin and Boden, 1833), loc. 53–124 of 268, Kindle. Idiosyncrasies original.

2. Richard S. Newman, *Freedom's Prophet: Bishop Richard Allen, the AME Church, and the Black Founding Fathers* (New York: New York University Press, 2008), 12–13.

3. Newman, *Freedom's Prophet*, 13.

4. Joanna Brooks, "The Early American Public Sphere and the Emergence of a Black Print Counterpublic," *William and Mary Quarterly*, 3rd ser., 62, no. 1 (January 2005): 81.

5. Newman, *Freedom's Prophet*, 116.

6. Edwin Black, "Excerpts from *Rhetorical Criticism: A Study in Method*," in *Readings in Rhetorical Criticism*, 5th ed., ed. Carl R. Burgchardt and Hillary A. Jones (State College: Strata, 2017), 51.

7. Burke, *Permanence and Change*, 90.

8. Sonja K. Foss, *Rhetorical Criticism: Exploration and Practice* (Prospect Heights, IL: Waveland Press, 1989), 367.

9. Foss, *Rhetorical Criticism*, 367.

10. Foss, *Rhetorical Criticism*, 368.

11. Foss, *Rhetorical Criticism*, 369.

12. The first is a self-reference to the autobiography itself. This reference stands on its own and does not add any clarity to our understanding of the word usage elsewhere.

13. Allen, *Rt. Rev. Richard Allen*, loc. 126 of 268.

14. Allen, *Rt. Rev. Richard Allen*, loc. 28 of 268. Allen felt the need to prove this to his owner because slaveholders often emphasized biblical texts that justified master-over-slave hierarchies. Allen needed, therefore, to demonstrate the truthfulness of his commitment by submitting to his master, even though his owner, at the time, did not express Christian faith or morality.

15. Allen, *Rt. Rev. Richard Allen*, loc. 41 of 268. Allen's owner, Sturgis, was in constant debt and had already sold several of Allen's family members. Dennis Dickerson, *African Methodism and Its Wesleyan Heritage: Reflections on AME Church History* (Nashville, TN: AME Publishing House, 2009), 19.

16. Dickerson, *African Methodism*, 20.

17. Gary B. Nash, "New Light on Richard Allen: The Early Years of Freedom," *William and Mary Quarterly* 46, no. 2 (April 1989): 333.

18. Allen, *Rt. Rev. Richard Allen*, loc. 53 of 268.

19. Allen, *Rt. Rev. Richard Allen*, loc. 53 of 268.

20. Allen, *Rt. Rev. Richard Allen*, loc. 114 of 268.

21. Heschel, *Prophets*, 34.

22. Allen, *Rt. Rev. Richard Allen*, loc. 66–75 of 268.

23. Burke, *Permanence and Change*, 134. See also Joel Overall, "Piano and Pen: Music as Kenneth Burke's Secular Conversion," *Rhetoric Society Quarterly* 41, no. 5 (2011), 439–54.

24. Christine D. Pohl, *Making Room: Recovering Hospitality as a Christian Tradition* (Grand Rapids, MI: William B. Eerdmans, 1999), 5.

25. Gal. 4:13–14 (NRSV): "You know that it was because of a physical infirmity that I first announced the gospel to you; though my condition put you to the test, you did not scorn or despise me, but welcomed me as an angel of God, as Christ Jesus."

26. See Gal. 1:13–2:10.

27. Rom. 10:15 (NRSV): "And how are they to proclaim him unless they are sent? As it is written, 'How beautiful are the feet of those who bring good news!'"

28. Allen, *Rt. Rev. Richard Allen*, loc. 73 of 268.

29. Allen, *Rt. Rev. Richard Allen*, loc. 55, 67, 91, 92 of 268.

30. Allen, *Rt. Rev. Richard Allen*, loc. 196 of 268.

31. One exception to this may be the resistance of some Black middle-class church audiences.

32. Exod. 3:11–12; Jer. 1:8.

33. 1 Sam. 3:19.

34. Acts 18:1–4 (NRSV):

After this Paul left Athens and went to Corinth. There he found a Jew named Aquila, a native of Pontus, who had recently come from Italy with his wife Priscilla, because Claudius had ordered all Jews to leave Rome. Paul went to see them, and, because he was of the same trade, he stayed with them, and they worked together—by trade they were tentmakers. Every sabbath he would argue in the synagogue and would try to convince Jews and Greeks.

35. Allen, *Rt. Rev. Richard Allen*, loc. 186, 227, 191 of 268.

36. Allen, *Rt. Rev. Richard Allen*, loc. 194 of 268.

37. Allen, *Rt. Rev. Richard Allen*, loc. 93 of 268.

38. Dickerson, *African Methodism*, 21.

39. Allen, *Rt. Rev. Richard Allen*, loc. 80 of 268.

40. Foss, *Rhetorical Criticism*, 369.

41. Duncan, introduction to *Permanence and Change*, xxxi.

42. Burke, *Permanence and Change*, 25.

43. Burke, *Permanence and Change*, 35.

44. Isa. 6:3 (AV).

45. Heschel, *Who Is Man?*, 93.

46. Newman, *Freedom's Prophet*, 119.

47. Asante, *Afrocentric Idea*, 48.

48. Newman, *Freedom's Prophet*, 23. Overlooked by scholars who assume a secular-sacred dichotomy, "Allen's life exemplified one of the defining characteristics of black activism before the Civil War: the movement from integrationist to nationalist beliefs. Perhaps because most scholars have viewed Allen as primarily a religious figure, his radical side has not garnered much attention." Ibid., 20.

49. Myers, *God's Yes*, 73.

50. Hobson, *Mount of Vision*, 155.

51. "Piety is a schema of orientation since it involves the putting together of experiences. The orientation may be right or wrong; it can guide or misguide." Burke, *Permanence and Change*, 76.

52. Burke, *Permanence and Change*, 94.

53. Dianna N. Watkins-Dickerson, "'You Are Somebody': A Study of the Prophetic Rhetoric of Rev. Henry Logan Starks, DMin," *Journal of Communication and Religion* 43, no. 4 (Winter 2020): 97.

54. Asante, *Afrocentric Idea*, 17.

55. "Often ignorant of African philosophy and culture, commentators have imposed Western constructs and values on material that grows out of coherent, albeit different, traditions." Asante, *Afrocentric Idea*, 25.

CHAPTER 3. THE CALL NARRATIVE OF JULIA FOOTE

1. Julia Foote, *A Brand Plucked from the Fire: An Autobiographical Sketch* (Cleveland: W. F. Schneider, 1879), 65–67.

2. Chanta M. Haywood, *Prophesying Daughters: Black Women Preachers and the Word, 1823–1913*, rev. ed. (Columbia: University of Missouri Press, 2003), 1.

3. Haywood, *Prophesying Daughters*, 14.

4. Foote, *Brand*, 65.

5. Foote, *Brand*, 65.

6. Foote, *Brand*, 78.

7. Foote, *Brand*, 67.

8. George Foote told her he would consider admitting her to an insane asylum if she began preaching. Foote, *Brand*, 67.

9. Her mother told her she would rather her daughter die than take up a preaching ministry. Foote, *Brand*, 84.

10. Her pastor and church threatened her with excommunication and church discipline. Foote, *Brand*, 102.

11. Heschel, *Prophets*, 31. Emphasis original.

12. Gafney, *Daughters of Miriam*, 111.

13. Kimberly P. Johnson, *The Womanist Preacher: Proclaiming Womanist Rhetoric from the Pulpit* (Lanham, MD: Lexington Books, 2017), xviii.

14. Sallie M. Cuffee, "Reconstructing Subversive Moral Discourses in the Spiritual Autobiographies of Nineteenth-Century African American Preaching Women," *Journal of Feminist Studies in Religion* 32, no. 2 (Fall 2016): 54.

15. K. Johnson, *Womanist Preacher*, xxi.

16. Kate Hanch, *Storied Witness: The Theology of Black Women Preachers in 19th-Century America* (Minneapolis, MN: Fortress Press, 2022), 3.

17. Cuffe, "Reconstructing Subversive Moral Discourses," 59.

18. Melbourne S. Cummings and Judi Moore Latta, "When They Honor the Voice: Centering African American Women's Call Stories," *Journal of Black Studies* 40, no. 4 (March 2010): 671.

19. Alice Walker, *In Search of Our Mother's Gardens* (San Diego: Harcourt Brace Jovanovich, 1983), xi–xii.

20. Cuffe, "Reconstructing Subversive Moral Discourses," 56.

21. K. Johnson, *Womanist Preacher*, 59.

22. Elisabeth Schussler Fiorenza, *But She Said: Feminist Practices of Biblical Interpretation* (Boston, MA: Beacon Press, 1992), 62.

23. K. Johnson, "Take the Man," 186.

24. Emilie M. Townes, *Womanist Justice, Womanist Hope*, American Academy of Religion Academy Series 79 (Atlanta, GA: Scholars Press, 1993), 188.

25. Annette D. Madlock, "Introduction to the Special Issue," in "A Womanist Rhetorical Vision for Building the Beloved Community," ed. Annette D. Madlock, special issue, *Journal of Communication and Religion* 43, no. 3 (Fall 2020): 6.

26. Katie Geneva Cannon, *Katie's Canon: Womanism and the Soul of the Black Community* (New York: Continuum, 1995), 56.

27. Elaine M. Flake, *God in Her Midst: Preaching Healing to Wounded Women* (Valley Forge: Judson Press, 2007), xiii.

28. Cummings and Latta, "Honor the Voice," 671.

29. K. Johnson, *Womanist Preacher*, xix.

30. Stacey M. Floyd-Thomas, "Writing for Our Lives: Womanism as an Epistemological Revolution," introduction to *Deeper Shades of Purple*, edited by Stacey M. Floyd-Thomas (New York: New York University Press, 2006), 2.

31. V. K. Bhatia, *Analyzing Genre: Language Use in Professional Settings* (London: Longman, 1993), 13.

32. R. Jones, *Discourse Analysis*, 10.

33. Cuffe, "Reconstructing Subversive Moral Discourses," 47.

34. Rodney H. Jones continues, "Genres do not only link people together; they also link people with certain activities, identities, roles and responsibilities." R. Jones, *Discourse Analysis*, 11.

35. William L. Andrews, *To Tell a Free Story: The First Century of Afro-American Autobiography, 1760–1865* (Urbana: University of Illinois Press, 1986), 1–2.

36. Katie Geneva Cannon, *Black Womanist Ethics* (New York: Oxford University Press, 1998), 76.

37. Stephen Kantrowitz, *More Than Freedom: Fighting for Black Citizenship in a White Republic, 1829–1889* (New York: Penguin Press, 2012), 5.

38. Brooks, "Early American Public Sphere," 70.

39. John Ernest, *Liberation Historiography: African American Writers and the Challenge of History, 1794–1861* (Chapel Hill: North Carolina University Press, 2004), 186.

40. McDonald, "From Resistance to Receiving," 220.

41. Cummings and Latta, "Honor the Voice," 667.

42. Cummings and Latta, "Honor the Voice," 671.

43. Foote, *Brand*, 65.

44. Hoyt, "Interpreting Biblical Scholarship," 25.

45. Barr, *Making of Biblical Womanhood*, 45.

46. Robert J. Patterson, "A Triple-Twined Re-appropriation: Womanist Theology and Gendered-Racial Protest in the Writings of Jarena Lee, Frances E. W. Harper, and Harriet Jacobs," *Religion and Literature* 45, no. 2 (Summer 2013): 57.

47. Hanch, *Storied Witness*, 70.

48. Hanch, *Storied Witness*, 71.

49. Patterson, "Triple-Twined Re-appropriation," 58.

50. *Soteriology* refers to the doctrine of salvation. It seeks to explain how God brings about salvation and restoration to individuals, communities, and all creation.

51. James H. Cone, *Black Theology and Black Power* (Maryknoll: Orbis Books, 1997), 49.

52. William L. Andrews, introduction to *Sisters of the Spirit: Three Black Women's Autobiographies of the Nineteenth Century*, ed. William L. Andrews (Bloomington: Indiana University Press, 1986), 1.

53. Foote, *Brand*, 11.

54. Jocelyn Moody, *Sentimental Confession* (Athens: University of Georgia Press, 2001), 22.

55. *Order of salvation* refers to how salvation works in Christian theology.

56. Hanch, *Storied Witness*, 90.

57. John Wesley, *The Works of John Wesley*, 3rd ed., vol. 5 (London: Wesleyan Methodist Book Room, 1872), 203. Emphasis added.

58. Haywood, *Prophesying Daughters*, 2.

59. Andrews, introduction to *Sisters of the Spirit*, 15.

60. Cummings and Latta, "Honor the Voice," 676.

61. Foote, *Brand*, 71.

62. Foote, *Brand*, 72.

63. Myers, *God's Yes*, 47, 48.

64. Andrews, introduction to *Sisters of the Spirit*, 14.

65. Foote, *Brand*, 72.

66. Foote, *Brand*, 78.

67. Foote, *Brand*, 71.

68. Foote, *Brand*, 72.

69. "The challenge of knowledge, the claiming of human agency, the affirmation of one's own humanity created in the image of God are essential dimensions of womanist approaches to theological anthropology." Elaine Robinson, *Race and Theology* (Nashville, TN: Abingdon Press, 2012), 36. Kimberly P. Johnson also notes that this is an aspect of womanist preaching as the preacher "culturally critiques the black church, the black community, and the oppressive aspects of this nation that continue to restrict women." K. Johnson, *Womanist Preacher*, 115–16.

70. R. Jones, *Discourse Analysis*, 104.

71. Future orientation is a result of the genre, not an inherent aspect of it. The future orientation arises out of the genre's desire to communicate that the universe will balance itself under God's justice. When a past orientation is more useful, as we will see later with Foote's use of Edenic imagery, apocalyptic rhetoric is equally comfortable there. After all, in the biblical apocalyptic genre, the future orientation is always to the pristine, Edenic past restored.

72. Barry Brummett, *Contemporary Apocalyptic Rhetoric* (New York: Praeger, 1991), 9–10.

73. David Bobbitt and Harold Mixon, "Prophecy and Apocalypse in the Rhetoric of Martin Luther King, Jr.," *Journal of Communication and Religion* 17, no. 1 (March 1994): 30.

74. Bobbitt and Mixon, "Prophecy and Apocalypse," 30.

75. Martin Luther King Jr., "I Have a Dream," 1967, National Mall, Washington, DC, quoted in Bobbitt and Mixon, "Prophecy and Apocalypse," 33. Emphasis added.

76. Though, she might say the genre *chose her.*

77. K. Johnson, *Womanist Preacher*, 115–16.

78. Foote, *Brand*, 70.

79. Gen. 3:6.

80. Flake, *God in Her Midst*, xiv.

81. Flake, *God in Her Midst*, 13–21.

82. Foote, *Brand*, 70.

83. John 13:1 (NRSV).

84. Cuffe, "Reconstructing Subversive Moral Discourses," 52.

85. Foote, *Brand*, 9.

86. Multiple times, Foote references apocalyptic visions when she feels that the threat of hell looms over her for her refusal to obey the angelic message.

87. Tamura Lomax, *Jezebel Unhinged: Loosing the Black Female Body in Religion and Culture* (Durham, NC: Duke University Press, 2018), "Introduction," loc. 381 of 6774, Kindle.

88. Hanch, *Storied Witness*, 110.

89. Cuffe, "Reconstructing Subversive Moral Discourses," 47.

90. Patricia Collins, "What's in a Time: Womanism, Black Feminism, and Beyond," *Black Scholar* 26 (1996): 9–17.

CHAPTER 4. THE CALL NARRATIVE OF NAT TURNER

1. Thomas R. Gray and Nat Turner, *The Confessions of Nat Turner* (Baltimore: Lucas and Deaver, 1831), DigitalCommons, University of Nebraska—Lincoln, accessed May 24, 2024, https://digitalcommons.unl.edu/cgi/viewcontent.cgi?article=1014&context=etas. 9–11. Idiosyncrasies original.

2. Makungu M. Akinyela, "Battling the Serpent: Nat Turner, Africanized Christianity, and a Black Ethos," *Journal of Black Studies* 33, no. 3 (January 2003): 259.

3. Nicholas May, "Holy Rebellion: Religious Assembly Laws in Antebellum South Carolina and Virginia," *American Journal of Legal History* 49, no. 3 (July 2007): 237.

4. Akinyela, "Battling the Serpent," 261. These doctrines demonstrate the universal depravity of humanity and therefore the imperfection of and limitations on slave owners' authority. They also display a series of messianic figures whose lives and rhetoric challenge unjust authorities. Further, they discuss a God who sides with slaves over masters, displaying his allegiance to *them* by resurrecting the dead.

5. A. J. Raboteau, *Slave Religion: The Invisible Institution in the American South* (Oxford: Oxford University Press, 1978), 132.

6. Kevin Pelletier, "David Walker, Harriet Beecher Stowe, and the Logic of Sentimental Terror," *African American Review* 46, no. 2–3 (Summer–Fall 2013): 260.

7. Akinyela, "Battling the Serpent," 256.

8. In 1739 in Charleston, South Carolina, sixty to one hundred enslaved people destroyed property and killed white people indiscriminately. The Stono Rebellion fostered a culture of fear of further violence in the South. The Stono events were explicitly tied to religion with the insurrectionists intentionally choosing Sunday because (1) it was enslaved people's day off, (2) the white enslavers were in church and defenseless, and (3) it represented a day of resurrection—release from bondage in the Christian tradition. May, "Holy Rebellion," 242.

9. In Richmond, Virginia, thousands of enslaved, highly skilled artisans, led by Gabrielle Prosser, plotted to kidnap the governor. Utilizing religious assemblies to recruit and train his followers, Prosser appealed to biblical texts to energize his troops and criticize oppressors. The fallout was the Slave Religion Law in South Carolina that forbade gatherings of enslaved persons for religious purposes. Virginia also used laws to target the religious gatherings of enslaved persons. There are questions about how well these laws were enforced. May, "Holy Rebellion," 247.

10. In Charleston, South Carolina, Vesey, a freeman, recruited among the enslaved population around Charleston. The conspiracy was exposed before it could be enacted, and the city of Charleston charged 131 people. Vesey's rationale was entirely religious and demonstrated to white enslavers the undeniable connection between the Black church and slave rebellions. Akinyela, "Battling the Serpent," 261.

11. Steven H. Shiffrin, "The Rhetoric of Black Violence in the Antebellum Period: Henry Highland Garnet," *Journal of Black Studies* 2, no. 1 (September 1971): 45–53.

12. May, "Holy Rebellion," 242.

13. Nancy Bullock Woolridge, "The Slave Preacher—Portrait of a Leader," *Journal of Negro Education* 14, no. 1 (Winter 1945): 28.

14. Woolridge, "Slave Preacher," 32.

15. May, "Holy Rebellion," 243.

16. Kantrowitz, *More Than Freedom*, 28.

17. David S. Cecelski, *The Fire of Freedom: Abraham Galloway and the Slaves' Civil War* (Chapel Hill: University of North Carolina Press, 2012), 10.

18. "In the wake of Nat Turner's rebellion in 1831 in Southampton County, Virginia, and in response to fears of slave insurrections, in 1832 the Maryland legislature proposed a statute to remove all free blacks from the state. The bill required manumitted slaves to renounce their freedom if they wished to stay behind with their families." Catherine Clinton, *Harriet Tubman: The Road to Freedom* (New York: Hachette Book Group, 2004), 34.

19. Martha S. Jones, *Birthright Citizens: A History of Race and Rights in Antebellum America* (Cambridge: Cambridge University Press, 2018), 79.

20. May, "Holy Rebellion," 252.

21. Stephen B. Oates, *The Fires of Jubilee: Nat Turner's Fierce Rebellion* (New York: HarperCollins, 1990), 14.

22. Randolf Ferguson Scully, "'I Come Here Before You and I Shall Not Go Away': Race, Gender, and Evangelical Community on the Eve of the Nat Turner Rebellion," *Journal of the Early Republic* 27, no. 4 (Winter 2007): 662.

23. "The revolt of enslaved Africans led by Nat Turner in 1931 was preceded by several years of political and economic uncertainty in the southern United States and a rapidly

changing international situation that had a direct effect on the U.S. economy and slave system." Akinyela, "Battling the Serpent," 260.

24. Seymour L. Gross and Eileen Bender, "History, Politics, and Literature: The Myth of Nat Turner," *American Quarterly* 23, no. 4 (October 1971): 493.

25. Daniel S. Fabricant, "Thomas R. Gray and William Styron: Finally, A Critical Look at the 1831 Confessions of Nat Turner," *American Journal of Legal History* 37, no. 3 (July 1993): 332–61.

26. Asante, *Afrocentric Idea*, 144.

27. Asante, *Afrocentric Idea*, 144. Emphasis added.

28. Asante is not alone in this. Thomas Gray appeared unsure of whether Turner believed his own story, and commentators at the time (James Trezevant, William Parker) questioned Turner's sanity. David F. Allmendinger Jr., *Nat Turner and the Rising in South Hampton County* (Baltimore, MD: John Hopkins University Press, 2014), 23.

29. N. Taylor, *Driven toward Madness*, 119.

30. "Then on August 13, the sun rose with a strange greenish tint; later, it turned to blue, and in the afternoon a dark spot was visible on its surface. The Richmond *Whig* reported that this occurrence 'stimulated' the slaves' 'religious devotion,' but to Turner it was a new sign, and according to one contemporary account he told his followers, 'as the black spot passed over the sun, so shall the blacks pass over the earth.'" Eric Foner, comp., *Nat Turner: Great Lives Observed* (Englewood Cliffs: Prentice-Hall, 1971), 3.

31. "Indeed they went on to revise and implement the slave codes in order to restrict blacks so stringently that they could never again mount a revolt. The revised laws not only strengthened the militia and patrol systems, but virtually stripped free Negroes of human rights and all but eliminated slave schools, slave religious meetings, and slave preachers. For Nat Turner had taught white Virginians a hard lesson about what might happen if they gave slaves enough education and a religion to think for themselves." Oates, *Fires of Jubilee*, 140.

32. May, "Holy Rebellion," 252.

33. Steven Taylor, "The Political Influence of African American Ministers: A Legacy of West African Culture," *Journal of Black Studies* 37, no. 1 (September 2006): 7.

34. Nat Turner, *"The Confessions of Nat Turner" and Related Documents*, ed. Kenneth S. Greenberg (Boston, MA: St. Martin's Press, 1996), 110.

35. Gross and Bender, "History, Politics, and Literature," 487.

36. I focus on this section of the narrative for two reasons: (1) I hope to make this part of a larger work on African American prophetic-call narratives, and (2) it provides a nice pericope with minimal text-critical problems other than those inherent to the text as a whole.

37. Burke, *Rhetoric of Motives*, 20–23.

38. Burke, *Rhetoric of Motives*, 22.

39. Maurice Charland, "Constitutive Rhetoric: The Case of the Peuple Quebecois," *Quarterly Journal of Speech* 73, no. 2 (1987): 133.

40. A. Johnson, "Prophetic Persona," 274. Emphasis added.

41. Delindus R. Brown and Wanda F. Anderson, "A Survey of the Black Woman and the Persuasion Process: The Study of Strategies of Identification and Resistance," *Journal of Black Studies* 9, no. 2 (December 1978): 233–48.

42. Brown and Anderson, "Survey," 235.

43. Glen McClish, "William G. Allen's 'Orators and Oratory': Inventional Amalgamation, Pathos, and the Characterization of Violence in African-American Abolitionist Rhetoric," *Rhetoric Society Quarterly* 35, no. 1 (Winter 2005): 63.

44. This was done through special efforts to "maintain blacks in a state of ignorance," "muzzling the oral communication of slaves," and prescribing "servile behavior for all blacks." Cal M. Logue, "Transcending Coercion: The Communicative Strategies of Black Slaves on Antebellum Plantations," *Quarterly Journal of Speech* 67, no. 1 (1981): 33–35.

45. Brown and Anderson, "Survey," 243. This invisibility, however, allows women to avoid the burden of open argumentation with the oppressor and make the most of their minimal social opportunities within an oppressive milieu.

46. Asante, *Afrocentric Idea*, 151.

47. M. Cooper Harriss, "Where Is the Voice Coming From? Rhetoric, Religion, and Violence in *The Confession of Nat Turner*," *Soundings: An Interdisciplinary Journal* 89, no. 1–2 (Spring–Summer 2006): 150.

48. Scully, "I Come Here," 664.

49. Donald G. Matthews, *Religion in the Old South* (Chicago: University of Chicago Press, 1977), 223, quoted in Wayne K. Durrill, "Nat Turner and Signs of the Apocalypse," in *Varieties of Southern Religious History: Essays in Honor of Donald G. Matthews*, ed. Regina D. Sullivan and Monte Harrell Hampton (Columbia: University of South Carolina Press, 2015), 78.

50. Pelletier, "David Walker," 257.

51. "And while no evidence exists that he ever read or even heard about Walker's *Appeal*, Nat felt the same frustrations that Walker did and was swept up in similar religious and revolutionary fervor." Oates, *Fires of Jubilee*, 51. Or as Vincent Harding says it, "No record exists of that contact, if it ever occurred. But the contact was not necessary, for Nat Turner had long been convinced that the God of Walker's *Appeal* had always been in Southampton." Vincent Harding, "Symptoms of Liberty and Blackhead Signposts: David Walker and Nat Turner," in *Nat Turner: A Slave Rebellion in History and Memory*, ed. Kenneth S. Greenberg (Oxford: Oxford University Press, 2002), 96.

52. Pelletier, "David Walker," 261.

53. Pelletier, "David Walker," 255.

54. James Jasinski, *Sourcebook on Rhetoric* (Thousand Oaks: SAGE, 2001); Darsey, *Prophetic Tradition*; Steven D. O'Leary, "A Dramatistic Theory of Apocalyptic Rhetoric," *Quarterly Journal of Speech* 79 (1999): 385–426.

55. Wayne K. Durrill attempts to explain all of Turner's apocalyptic visions naturalistically. While we can appreciate the seriousness with which he takes Turner's claims, I doubt Turner would understand his apocalyptic encounters in this way. Durrill, "Nat Turner."

56. Stephen Howard Browne, "'This Unparalleled and Inhumane Massacre': The Gothic, the Sacred, and the Meaning of Nat Turner," *Rhetoric and Public Affairs* 3, no. 3 (Fall 2000): 326.

57. For example, "Behold me as I stand in the heavens" explicitly references the prophet Isaiah's apocalyptic vision of the messianic kingdom wherein "the servants, formerly hungry and thirsty, shall be fed and shall drink; the crimes of the society, which will be erased when 'a new heavens and a new earth' are created, 'shall not be remembered, nor come to mind.'"

Anthony Santoro, "The Prophet in His Own Words: Nat Turner's Biblical Construction," *Virginia Magazine of History and Biography* 116, no. 2 (2008): 126. Neither Isaiah's words nor Turner's employment of them assume apocalypse points to anything other than this-worldly events. Apocalypse certainly contains heavenly visions, but those visions almost always provide some meaning or impetus for action on earth.

58. James Sidbury, "Reading, Revelation, and Rebellion: The Textual Communities of Gabriel, Denmark Vesey, and Nat Turner," in *Nat Turner: A Slave Rebellion in History and Memory*, ed. Kenneth S. Greenberg (Oxford: Oxford University Press, 2002), 126.

59. A cursory reading of *The Confessions* finds several apocalyptic citations from Paul, Ezek., Joel 2, Acts 2, and Rev. 5.

60. Asante, *Afrocentric Idea*, 144.

61. Asante, *Afrocentric Idea*, 144.

62. "Gray picked up fees as defense counsel, but they were not the main chance, as he saw it. *The Confessions* were." Anthony E. Kaye, "Neighborhoods and Nat Turner: The Making of a Slave Rebel and the Unmaking of a Slave Rebellion," *Journal of the Early Republic* 27, no. 4 (Winter 2007): 708. In fact, "All told, the *Confessions* sold about forty thousand copies, although some Southern communities appear to have suppressed it, presumably because of its 'incendiary' character." Oates, *Fires of Jubilee*, 144–45. Gray apparently needed the money: "At the time of Turner's rebellion, the thirty-one-year-old Gray was a man in desperate financial need, a man on the edge of failure as a planter." Turner, *Confessions of Nat Turner*, 8.

63. Browne, "Unparalleled and Inhumane Massacre," 311.

64. Logue, "Transcending Coercion," 39.

65. Turner, *Confessions of Nat Turner*, 9.

66. Santoro, "Prophet," 116.

67. Gross and Bender, "History, Politics, and Literature," 493. We must ask, as well, whether such an effort was even needed. The newspapers at the time were already making this case and shaping public imagination. For example, on August 24, 1831, the *Richmond Compiler* described Turner as "mad—infatuated—deceived by some artful knaves, or stimulated by their own miscalculating passions." Turner, *Confessions of Nat Turner*, 61. Further, if Gray's goal was to assuage anxiety, saying Turner and his actions "curdled" the blood in his veins hardly seems like an effective rhetorical tactic.

68. May, "Holy Rebellion," 255.

69. May, "Holy Rebellion," 255.

70. "Gray displayed no scriptural fluency like that in the memoir. He neither identified the passages nor drew attention to the allegory. Those sections of the *Confessions* written in his own voice lack the religious sensibility of the memoir." Allmendinger, *Nat Turner*, 248.

71. The account on November 4, 1831, of Turner's capture in the *Norfolk Herald* discusses Turner's commitment to his prophetic status and his insistence on the validity of his apocalyptic visions. It also suggests the importance of Turner's religious authority for maintaining "complete control over his followers." Turner, *Confessions of Nat Turner*, 90.

72. Pelletier, "David Walker," 258.

73. Gray and Turner, *Confessions of Nat Turner*, 22.

74. Eric J. Sundquist, *To Wake the Nations: Race in the Making of American Literature* (Cambridge, MA: Harvard University Press, 1993), 37.

75. Sundquist, *To Wake the Nations*, 49.

76. Scully, "I Come Here," 665.

77. Scully, "I Come Here," 666.

78. Eugene D. Genovese, "William Styron's *The Confessions of Nat Turner*: A Meditation on Evil, Redemption, and History," in *Novel History: Historians and Novelists Confront America's Past (and Each Other)*, ed. Mark C. Carnes (New York: Simon and Schuster, 2001), 210–11.

79. In fact, the rhetorical efficacy of *The Confessions* makes it worthy of study regardless of how clearly or unclearly Turner's voice comes through. The text has provided fodder for nearly two centuries of Black nationalists and militant resistors.

80. Browne, "Unparalleled and Inhumane Massacre," 315.

81. This becomes evident in Turner's religious seriousness, his moral convictions not to participate in thievery, like his contemporaries did, his submission to his enslaver and eventual return after running away, his attendance at church, and his meditation on scripture. All these values were held in high regard by white Christian enslavers.

82. Browne, "Unparalleled and Inhumane Massacre," 325.

83. Carlacio, "Speaking," chap. 8, loc. 1686 of 3818.

84. Melbourne S. Cummings, "Problems of Researching Black Rhetoric," *Journal of Black Studies* 2, no. 4 (June 1972): 504.

85. Cummings, "Researching Black Rhetoric," 505.

86. Herbert A. Wichelns, "The Literary Criticism of Oratory," in *The Rhetorical Idiom: Essays in Rhetoric, Oratory, Language, and Drama*, ed. Donald C. Bryant (Ithaca: Cornell University Press, 1958), 38–39.

87. "What counts as fact, as relevant, as sufficiently interesting to merit publication, was of course determined by the audience—and white curiosity and self-interested benevolence in the story of African American character was a significant and, more often than not, distorting presence." Ernest, *Liberation Historiography*, 164.

88. "African American criminality became one of the most widely accepted bases for justifying prejudicial thinking, discriminatory treatment, and/or acceptance of racial violence as an instrument of public safety." Khalil Gibran Muhammad, *The Condemnation of Blackness: Race, Crime, and the Making of Modern Urban America* (Cambridge, MA: Harvard University Press, 2010), 4.

89. "African tradition held that a male with markings like these was destined to become a leader." Oates, *Fires of Jubilee*, 12.

90. Asante, *Afrocentric Idea*, 147.

91. Scully, "I Come Here," 670.

92. Celucien L. Joseph, "Toward a Black African Theological Anthropology and Ubuntu Ethics," *Journal of Religion and Theology* 2, no. 1 (2018): 27.

93. Luke 1:46–55.

94. The ability to read itself would have been a subversive skill given that slave owners forbade their slaves to learn to read. By suggesting that his literacy originates in supernatural gifting, Turner employs conscious identification. He knows the oppressors' desire and justification for keeping slaves illiterate, but by claiming supernatural origins, Turner is able to

resist those desires and cast a vision for other enslaved persons of a God who wishes to free them from the restraints of white Christian oppression.

95. Asante, *Afrocentric Idea*, 142.

96. Jeffrey Ogbonna Green Ogbar, "Prophet Nat and God's Children of Darkness: Black Religious Nationalism," *Journal of Religious Thought* 53–54, no. 2–1 (1991): 52.

97. Matt. 4:1–11.

98. Gray and Turner, *Confessions of Nat Turner*, 9. Turner does not cite the entirety of Matt. 6:33 (here, AV): "But seek ye first the kingdom of God, *and his righteousness*; and all *these* things shall be added unto you." Emphasis added.

99. Gray and Turner, *Confessions of Nat Turner*, 9.

100. Asante, *Afrocentric Idea*, 139.

101. Gray and Turner, *Confessions of Nat Turner*, 11.

102. James H. Cone, *The Cross and the Lynching Tree* (Maryknoll: Orbis Press, 2011), 86.

103. "Nat's identification with the crucified Christ refigures the New Testament Jesus, and inscribes a *newer testament* of God's revelation to humankind in the history of salvation." Harriss, "Where Is the Voice," 156.

104. Harding, "Symptoms of Liberty," 80.

105. All throughout the biblical narrative, the name of God chosen by the various narrators always has some significance. For God to reveal God's self as "the Almighty" prefigures the apocalyptic scenario Turner later envisions and provides the kind of hopeful energy necessary for a prophet to announce the overthrowing of a powerful empire.

106. Gray and Turner, *Confessions of Nat Turner*, 8.

107. Asante, *Afrocentric Idea*, 143.

108. Gray and Turner, *Confessions of Nat Turner*, 10.

109. Andre E. Johnson proposed this insight after reading the original draft of this chapter.

110. Gray and Turner, *Confessions of Nat Turner*, 10.

111. Gray and Turner, *Confessions of Nat Turner*, 10.

112. Ogbar, "Prophet Nat," 56.

113. Ogbar, "Prophet Nat," 56.

114. Asante, *Afrocentric Idea*, 141. Emphasis added.

115. Gray and Turner, *Confessions of Nat Turner*, 11.

116. Gray and Turner, *Confessions of Nat Turner*, 11.

117. Gray and Turner, *Confessions of Nat Turner*, 11.

118. "In seven of the revelations, according to the text, Turner said specifically that the Spirit was present as a voice; it spoke always in biblical language, and on four occasions it quoted scripture. Two appearances involved visions of the Holy Ghost, and one, simply a vision and a voice. Finally, in 1831, he witnessed two signs that the Spirit had told him would appear in the heavens." Allmendinger, *Nat Turner*, 15.

119. Allmendinger, *Nat Turner*, 684.

120. Adetokunbo F. Knowles-Borishade, "Paradigm for Classical African Orature: Instrument for a Scientific Revolution?," *Journal of Black Studies* 21, no. 4 (June 1991): 496.

121. Gray and Turner, *Confessions of Nat Turner*, 18.

122. Darsey, *Prophetic Tradition*, 33.

123. Darsey, *Prophetic Tradition*, 33.

124. Andre E. Johnson, *No Future in This Country: The Prophetic Pessimism of Bishop Henry McNeal Turner* (Jackson: University Press of Mississippi, 2020), 3–22.

125. Black, "Excerpts from *Rhetorical Criticism*," 51.

126. Charland, "Constitutive Rhetoric," 133.

127. Charland, "Constitutive Rhetoric," 133.

128. Isa. 6:9 (AV).

129. Heschel, *Prophets*, 22.

A PERILOUS CONCLUSION

1. Darsey, *Prophetic Tradition*, xi.

2. Robert H. Craig, review of *The Prophetic Tradition and Radical Rhetoric in America*, by James Darsey, *Journal of American History* 85, no. 2 (September 1998): 635.

3. Black, "Excerpts from *Rhetorical Criticism*," 51.

4. Quentin J. Schultze, "The 'God-Problem' in Communication Studies," *Journal of Communication and Religion* 28, no. 1 (March 2005): 1.

5. Schultze, "God-Problem," 1.

6. Cone, *Speaking the Truth*, 9.

7. Quentin J. Schultze, "The Nature and Future of Religious Communication Scholarship," *Journal of Communication and Religion* 33, no. 2 (November 2010): 193.

8. Schultze, again, highlights this: "What should we make of the fact that communication textbooks, for instance, assume that human beings themselves create meaning rather than discover at least some of it? Is there no meaning whatsoever outside of our minds and cultures?" Schultze, "God-Problem," 4.

9. Brian Kaylor, "Accounting for the Divine: Examining Rhetorical Claims of God's Inspiration," *Journal of Communication and Religion* 34, no. 1 (May 2011): 76.

10. Schultze, "God-Problem," 6.

11. Kaylor, "Accounting for the Divine," 82.

12. For example, Kaylor compares God to a boss (1) who provides motivation for a presentation, (2) who might attend a presentation, and (3) whose response might determine how the audience might also respond to the presentation. Kaylor, "Accounting for the Divine," 84. I add to this that in religious rhetoric, (4) God sometimes oversees the production, dictates the words, or even edits the presentation depending on the level of inspiration the rhetor claims.

13. Schultze, "God-Problem," 10.

14. Alston-Miller, "Pauline Epistles," 113.

15. Chaïm Perelman, "Reply to Stanley H. Rosen," *Inquiry* 2 (1959): 86, quoted in Frank, "Arguing with God," 72.

16. Darsey, *Prophetic Tradition*, 201.

17. Ernest, *Liberation Historiography*, 36.

18. Andy Crouch, *Playing God: Redeeming the Gift of Power* (Downers Grove: InterVarsity Press, 2003), 55.

19. Royster and Kirsch, *Feminist Rhetorical Practices*, loc. 183 of 2384.

20. Schultze, "God-Problem," 16.

21. Woodyard, "Depatriarchalizing in Rhetorical Theory," 37.

22. Lloyd F. Bitzer, "The Rhetorical Situation," in *Readings in Rhetorical Criticism*, 5th ed., ed. Carl R. Burgchardt and Hillary A. Jones (State College: Strata, 2017), 35.

23. Black, "Excerpts from *Rhetorical Criticism*," 45.

24. Black, "Excerpts from *Rhetorical Criticism*," 45.

25. Charland, "Constitutive Rhetoric," 133. Emphasis original.

26. Isa. 6:9–10 (AV).

27. Herbert A. Wichelns, "The Literary Criticism of Oratory," in *Readings in Rhetorical Criticism*, 5th ed., ed. Carl R. Burgchardt and Hillary A. Jones (State College: Strata, 2017), 22.

28. Darsey, *Prophetic Tradition*, 113.

29. Charland, "Constitutive Rhetoric," 133.

30. Heschel, *Prophets*, 22.

31. Karlyn Kohrs Campbell, "Stanton's 'The Solitude of Self': A Rationale for Feminism," *Quarterly Journal of Speech* 66, no. 3 (1980): 308.

32. Asante, *Afrocentric Idea*, 147.

33. Burke, *Permanence and Change*, 81.

34. Interestingly, Burke ends this quote with "if we are to forestall the concocting of similar medicine in America." He does not notice that such medicines had been served by the spoon of white supremacy in America for a few centuries. Kenneth Burke, "The Rhetoric of Hitler's 'Battle,'" in *Readings in Rhetorical Criticism*, 5th ed., ed. Carl R. Burgchardt and Hillary A. Jones (State College: Strata, 2017), 211.

35. Maulana Karenga, "Nommo, Kawaida, and Communicative Practice," in *Understanding African American Rhetoric: Classical Origins to Contemporary Innovations*, ed. Ronald L. Jackson and Elain B. Johnson (New York: Routledge, 2003), 6.

36. Vincent L. Wimbush, "Introduction: Interpretating Resistance, Resisting Interpretations," *Semeia* 79 (1997): 6.

37. Reggie L. Williams, *Bonhoeffer's Black Jesus: Harlem Renaissance Theology and an Ethic of Resistance* (Waco: Baylor University Press, 2014), 43.

38. Hall, *Faithful Account*, 18.

39. Von Rad, *Message of the Prophets*, 61.

40. M. Jones, *Birthright Citizens*, 72.

41. Royster and Kirsch, *Feminist Rhetorical Practices*, loc. 380 of 2384.

42. Campbell, "Rhetoric of Women's Liberation," 84.

43. Jacqueline Jones Royster, "Introduction: Marking Trails in Studies of Race, Gender, and Culture," in *Calling Cards: Theory and Practice in the Study of Race, Gender, and Culture*, ed. Jacqueline Jones Royster and Ann Marie Mann Simpkins (Albany: State University of New York Press, 2005), loc. 123 of 3818, Kindle.

44. Royster and Kirsch, *Feminist Rhetorical Practices*, loc. 43 of 2384.

45. Lomax, *Jezebel Unhinged*, chap. 3, loc. 1698 of 6774.

46. Royster and Kirsch, *Feminist Rhetorical Practices*, loc. 640 of 2384.

47. Knowles-Borishade, "Classical African Orature," 496.

48. Knowles-Borishade, "Classical African Orature," 498.

49. Royster and Kirsch, *Feminist Rhetorical Practices*, loc. 1977 of 2384.

50. Quintilian, *Quintilian on the Teaching of Speaking and Writing*, ed. James J. Murphy (Carbondale: Southern Illinois University Press, 1987), xviii. Later studies have demonstrated the classist nature of Quintilian's understanding of who "good" people can be and certainly the sexist nature of *goodness* only being applicable to "man." These are all valid critiques. I merely quote him here to show the depth and history of rhetoric's disciplinary moral commitments, even if those needed expansion and rethinking through the years.

51. Black, "Excerpts from *Rhetorical Criticism*," 49.

52. James F. Klumpp and Thomas A. Hollihan, "Rhetorical Criticism as Moral Action," *Quarterly Journal of Speech* 75, no. 1 (February 1989): 84–96.

53. Asante, *Afrocentric Idea*, 193.

54. Charland, "Constitutive Rhetoric," 133.

Bibliography

Akinyela, Makungu M. "Battling the Serpent: Nat Turner, Africanized Christianity, and a Black Ethos." *Journal of Black Studies* 33, no. 3 (January 2003), 255–80.

Allen, Richard. *The Life, Experience, and Gospel Labours of the Rt. Rev. Richard Allen*. Philadelphia, PA: Martin and Boden, 1833. Kindle.

Allmendinger, David F., Jr. *Nat Turner and the Rising in South Hampton County*. Baltimore, MD: John Hopkins University Press, 2014.

Alston-Miller, Monika R. "The Influence of the Pauline Epistles on Maria W. Stewart's Rhetoric: A Political Gospel." *Journal of Communication and Religion* 38, no. 2 (Summer 2015): 100–117.

Alter, Robert. *The Hebrew Bible: A Translation with Commentary*. Vol. 2, *Prophets*. New York: W. W. Norton, 2019.

Andrews, William L. Introduction to *Sisters of the Spirit: Three Black Women's Autobiographies of the Nineteenth Century*, edited by William L. Andrews, 1–22. Bloomington: Indiana University Press, 1986.

Andrews, William L. *To Tell a Free Story: The First Century of Afro-American Autobiography, 1760–1865*. Urbana: University of Illinois Press, 1986.

Asante, Molefi Kete. *The Afrocentric Idea*. Philadelphia, PA: Temple University Press, 1998.

Asante, Molefi Kete. "Maat and Human Communication: Supporting Identity, Culture, and History without Global Domination." *Intercultural Communication Studies* 20, no. 1 (2011): 49–56.

Barr, Beth Allison. *The Making of Biblical Womanhood: How the Subjugation of Women Became Gospel Truth*. Grand Rapids, MI: Brazos Press, 2021.

Bhatia, V. K. *Analyzing Genre: Language Use in Professional Settings*. London: Longman, 1993.

Bitzer, Lloyd F. "The Rhetorical Situation." In *Readings in Rhetorical Criticism*, 5th ed., edited by Carl R. Burgchardt and Hillary A. Jones, 33–41. State College: Strata, 2017.

Black, Edwin. "Excerpts from *Rhetorical Criticism: A Study in Method*." In *Readings in Rhetorical Criticism*, 5th ed., edited by Carl R. Burgchardt and Hillary A. Jones, 42–53. State College: Strata, 2017.

Black, Edwin. "The Second Persona." In *Contemporary Rhetorical Theory: A Reader*, 2nd ed., edited by Mark J. Porrovecchio and Celeste Michelle Condit, 54–63. New York: Guilford Press, 2016.

Block, Daniel I. *Judges, Ruth*. The New American Commentary 6. Nashville, TN: Broadman and Holman, 1999.

Bobbitt, David, and Harold Mixon. "Prophecy and Apocalypse in the Rhetoric of Martin
    Luther King, Jr." *Journal of Communication and Religion* 17, no. 1 (March 1994): 27–38.
Brooks, Joanna. "The Early American Public Sphere and the Emergence of a Black Print
    Counterpublic." *William and Mary Quarterly*, 3rd ser., 62, no. 1 (January 2005): 67–92.
Brown, Delindus R., and Wanda F. Anderson. "A Survey of the Black Woman and the
    Persuasion Process: The Study of Strategies of Identification and Resistance." *Journal of
    Black Studies* 9, no. 2 (December 1978): 233–48.
Browne, Stephen Howard. "'This Unparalleled and Inhumane Massacre': The Gothic, the
    Sacred, and the Meaning of Nat Turner." *Rhetoric and Public Affairs* 3, no. 3 (Fall 2000):
    309–31.
Brueggemann, Walter. *Genesis: Interpretation*. Louisville, KY: John Knox Press, 1982.
Brueggemann, Walter. *The Prophetic Imagination*. 2nd ed. Minneapolis, MN: Fortress Press,
    2001.
Brummett, Barry. *Contemporary Apocalyptic Rhetoric*. New York: Praeger, 1991.
Burke, Kenneth. *Language as Symbolic Action: Essays On Life, Literature and Method*.
    Berkeley: University of California, 1968.
Burke, Kenneth. *Permanence and Change: An Anatomy of Purpose*. Berkeley: University of
    California Press, 1984.
Burke, Kenneth. "The Rhetoric of Hitler's 'Battle.'" In *Readings in Rhetorical Criticism*, 5th
    ed., edited by Carl R. Burgchardt and Hillary A. Jones, 210–24. State College: Strata, 2017.
Burke, Kenneth. *A Rhetoric of Motives*. Berkley: University of California Press, 1969.
Campbell, Karlyn Kohrs. "The Rhetoric of Women's Liberation: An Oxymoron." *Quarterly
    Journal of Speech* 59, no. 1 (February 1973): 74–86.
Campbell, Karlyn Kohrs. "Stanton's 'The Solitude of Self': A Rationale for Feminism."
    Quarterly Journal of Speech 66, no. 3 (1980): 304–12.
Campbell, Karlyn Kohrs, and Kathleen Hall Jamieson. "Form and Genre in Rhetorical
    Criticism: An Introduction." In *Form and Genre: Shaping Rhetorical Action*, edited
    by Karlyn Kohrs Campbell and Kathleen Hall Jamieson, 9–32. Falls Church: Speech
    Communication Association, 1976.
Cannon, Katie Geneva. *Black Womanist Ethics*. New York: Oxford University Press, 1998.
Cannon, Katie Geneva. *Katie's Canon: Womanism and the Soul of the Black Community*.
    New York: Continuum, 1995.
Carlacio, Jamie L. "Speaking with and to Me: Discursive Positioning and the Unstable
    Categories of Race, Class, and Gender." In *Calling Cards: Theory and Practice in the
    Study of Race, Gender, and Culture*, edited by Jacqueline Jones Royster and Ann
    Marie Mann Simpkins. Albany: State University of New York Press, 2005. Kindle.
Cecelski, David S. *The Fire of Freedom: Abraham Galloway and the Slaves' Civil War*. Chapel
    Hill: University of North Carolina Press, 2012.
Charland, Maurice. "Constitutive Rhetoric: The Case of the Peuple Quebecois." *Quarterly
    Journal of Speech* 73, no. 2 (1987): 133–50.
Clinton, Catherine. *Harriet Tubman: The Road to Freedom*. New York: Hachette Book
    Group, 2004.
Collins, Patricia. "What's in a Time: Womanism, Black Feminism, and Beyond." *Black
    Scholar* 26 (1996): 9–17.

Cone, James H. *Black Theology and Black Power*. Maryknoll: Orbis Books, 1997.

Cone, James H. *The Cross and the Lynching Tree*. Maryknoll: Orbis Press, 2011.

Cone, James H. *Speaking the Truth: Ecumenism, Liberation, and Black Theology*. Grand Rapids, MI: Eerdmans, 1986.

Cooper, Valerie C. *Word, like Fire: Maria Stewart, the Bible, and the Rights of African Americans*. Charlottesville: University of Virginia Press, 2011.

Craig, Robert H. Review of *The Prophetic Tradition and Radical Rhetoric in America*, by James Darsey. *Journal of American History* 85, no. 2 (September 1998): 634–35.

Crouch, Andy. *Playing God: Redeeming the Gift of Power*. Downers Grove: InterVarsity Press, 2003.

Cuffee, Sallie M. "Reconstructing Subversive Moral Discourses in the Spiritual Autobiographies of Nineteenth-Century African American Preaching Women." *Journal of Feminist Studies in Religion* 32, no. 2 (Fall 2016): 45–62.

Cummings, Melbourne S. "Problems of Researching Black Rhetoric." *Journal of Black Studies* 2, no. 4 (June 1972): 503–8.

Cummings, Melbourne S., and Judi Moore Latta. "When They Honor the Voice: Centering African American Women's Call Stories." *Journal of Black Studies* 40, no. 4 (March 2010): 666–82.

Darsey, James. *The Prophetic Tradition and Radical Rhetoric in America*. New York: New York University Press, 1997.

DeSantis, Alan D. "An Amostic Prophecy: Frederick Douglass' *The Meaning of the Fourth of July for the Negro*." *Journal of Communication and Religion* 22, no. 1 (March 1999): 65–92.

Dickerson, Dennis. *African Methodism and Its Wesleyan Heritage: Reflections on AME Church History*. Nashville, TN: AME Publishing House, 2009.

Douglass, Frederick. "What to the Slave Is the Fourth of July?" July 5, 1892. Teaching American History. Accessed April 16, 2024. https://teachingamericanhistory.org/library/document/what-to-the-slave-is-the-fourth-of-july/.

Duarte, Nancy. *Resonate: Present Visual Stories That Transform Audiences*. Hoboken, NJ: John Wiley and Sons, 2010.

Du Bois, W. E. B. *The Souls of Black Folk*. New York: Cosimo Classics, 2007.

Duncan, Hugh Dalziel. Introduction to *Permanence and Change: An Anatomy of Purpose*, by Kenneth Burke, xiii–xliv. Berkeley: University of California Press, 1984.

Durrill, Wayne K. "Nat Turner and Signs of the Apocalypse." In *Varieties of Southern Religious History: Essays in Honor of Donald G. Matthews*, edited by Regina D. Sullivan and Monte Harrell Hampton, 77–93. Columbia: University of South Carolina Press, 2015.

Ernest, John. *Liberation Historiography: African American Writers and the Challenge of History, 1794–1861*. Chapel Hill: North Carolina University Press, 2004.

Fabricant, Daniel S. "Thomas R. Gray and William Styron: Finally, A Critical Look at the 1831 Confessions of Nat Turner." *American Journal of Legal History* 37, no. 3 (July 1993): 332–61.

Fiorenza, Elisabeth Schussler. *But She Said: Feminist Practices of Biblical Interpretation*. Boston, MA: Beacon Press, 1992.

Fisher, Walter R. "Narration as Human Communication Paradigm: The Case of Public Moral Argument." *Communication Monographs* 51, no. 1 (1984): 1–22.

Flake, Elaine M. *God in Her Midst: Preaching Healing to Wounded Women*. Valley Forge: Judson Press, 2007.

Floyd-Thomas, Stacey M. "Writing for Our Lives: Womanism as an Epistemological Revolution." Introduction to *Deeper Shades of Purple*, edited by Stacey M. Floyd-Thomas, 1–14. New York: New York University Press, 2006.

Foner, Eric, comp. *Nat Turner: Great Lives Observed*. Englewood Cliffs: Prentice Hall, 1971.

Foote, Julia. *A Brand Plucked from the Fire: An Autobiographical Sketch*. Cleveland: W. F. Schneider, 1879.

Foss, Sonja K. *Rhetorical Criticism: Exploration and Practice*. Prospect Heights, IL: Waveland Press, 1989.

Foss, Sonja K., and Cindy L. Griffin. "Beyond Persuasion: A Proposal for Invitational Rhetoric." In *Contemporary Rhetorical Theory: A Reader*, 2nd ed., edited by Mark J. Porrovecchio and Celeste Michelle Condit. New York: Guilford Press, 2016.

Frank, David A. "Arguing with God, Talmudic Discourse, and the Jewish Countermodel: Implications for the Study of Argumentation." *Argumentation and Advocacy* 41 (Fall 2004): 71–86.

Fuerst, Thomas M. "A King's Place Is in the Kitchen: The Rhetorical Trajectory of the Rev. Dr. Martin Luther King, Jr.'s Kitchen Table Experience." *Listening: Journal of Communication, Ethics, Religion, and Culture* 55, no. 3 (Fall 2020): 160–74.

Gafney, Wilda C. *Daughters of Miriam: Women Prophets in Ancient Israel*. Minneapolis, MN: Fortress Press, 2008.

Genovese, Eugene D. "William Styron's *The Confessions of Nat Turner*: A Meditation on Evil, Redemption, and History." In *Novel History: Historians and Novelists Confront America's Past (And Each Other)*, edited by Mark C. Carnes, 209–20. New York: Simon and Schuster, 2001.

Gittens, Rhana A. "'What If I Am a Woman?': Black Feminist Rhetorical Strategies of Intersectional Identification and Resistance in Maria Stewart's Texts." *Southern Communication Journal* 83, no. 5 (2018): 310–21.

Glaude, Eddie S., Jr. *Exodus! Religion, Race, and Nation in Early Nineteenth-Century Black America*. Chicago: University of Chicago Press, 2000.

Gray, Thomas R., and Nat Turner. *The Confessions of Nat Turner*. Baltimore: Lucas and Deaver, 1831.DigitalCommons. University of Nebraska—Lincoln. Accessed May 24, 2024. https://digitalcommons.unl.edu/cgi/viewcontent.cgi?article=1014&context=etas.

Gross, Seymour L., and Eileen Bender. "History, Politics, and Literature: The Myth of Nat Turner." *American Quarterly* 23, no 4 (October 1971): 487–518.

Habel, Norm. "The Form and Significance of the Call Narratives." *Zeitschrift für die alttestamentliche Wissenschaft* 77, no. 3 (1965): 297–323.

Hall, Stephen G. *A Faithful Account of the Race: African American Historical Writing in the Nineteenth Century*. Chapel Hill: University of North Carolina Press, 2009.

Hanch, Kate. *Storied Witness: The Theology of Black Women Preachers in 19th-Century America*. Minneapolis, MN: Fortress Press, 2022.

Harding, Vincent. "Symptoms of Liberty and Blackhead Signposts: David Walker and Nat Turner." In *Nat Turner: A Slave Rebellion in History and Memory*, edited by Kenneth S. Greenberg, 79–102. Oxford: Oxford University Press, 2002.

Harrel, Willie, Jr. "A Call to Political and Social Activism: The Jeremiadic Discourse of Maria Miller Stewart, 1831–1833." *Journal of International Women's Studies* 9, no. 3 (May 2008): 300–319.

Harriss, M. Cooper. "Where Is the Voice Coming From? Rhetoric, Religion, and Violence in *The Confession of Nat Turner.*" *Soundings: An Interdisciplinary Journal* 89, no. 1–2 (Spring–Summer 2006): 135–70.

Haywood, Chanta M. *Prophesying Daughters: Black Women Preachers and the Word, 1823–1913.* Rev. ed. Columbia: University of Missouri Press, 2003.

Heschel, Abraham J. *The Insecurity of Freedom: Essays on Human Existence.* New York: Schocken, 1972.

Heschel, Abraham J. *The Prophets.* New York: HarperCollins, 1962.

Heschel, Abraham J. *Who Is Man?* Stanford: Stanford University Press, 1965.

Hobson, Christopher Z. *The Mount of Vision: African American Prophetic Tradition, 1800–1950.* Oxford: Oxford University Press, 2012.

Hoyt, Thomas, Jr. "Interpreting Biblical Scholarship for the Black Church Tradition." In *The Stony Road We Trod*, edited by Cain Hope Felder, 17–39. Minneapolis, MN: Fortress Press, 1991.

Hughes, Richard T. *Myths America Lives By: White Supremacy and the Stories That Give Us Meaning.* Urbana: University of Illinois Press, 2018.

Jackson, Ronald L. "Afrocentricity as Metatheory: A Dialogic Exploration of Its Principles." In *Understanding African American Rhetoric: Classical Origins to Contemporary Innovations*, edited by Ronald L. Jackson and Elain B. Johnson, 115–29. New York: Routledge, 2003.

Japp, Phyllis M. "Esther or Isaiah? The Abolitionist-Feminist Rhetoric of Angelina Grimke." *Quarterly Journal of Speech* 71, no. 3 (1985): 335–48.

Jasinski, James. *Sourcebook on Rhetoric.* Thousand Oaks: SAGE, 2001.

Johnson, Andre E. *The Forgotten Prophet: Bishop Henry McNeal Turner and the African American Prophetic Tradition.* Lanham, MD: Lexington Books, 2012.

Johnson, Andre E. "Introduction." *Listening: Journal of Communication, Ethics, Religion, and Culture* 55, no. 3 (Fall 2020): 148–50.

Johnson, Andre E. *No Future in This Country: The Prophetic Pessimism of Bishop Henry McNeal Turner.* Jackson: University Press of Mississippi, 2020.

Johnson, Andre E. "The Prophetic Persona of James Cone and the Rhetorical Theology of Black Theology." *Black Theology: An International Journal* 8, no. 3 (2010): 266–85.

Johnson, Andre E. "'To Make the World So Damn Uncomfortable': W. E. B. Du Bois and the African American Prophetic Tradition." *Carolinas Communication Annual* 32 (2016): 16–29.

Johnson, Kimberly P. "'Must Thee Take the Man Exclusively': Jarena Lee and Claiming the Right to Preach." *Listening: Journal of Communication Ethics, Religion, and Culture* 55, no. 3 (Fall 2020): 181–94.

Johnson, Kimberly P. *The Womanist Preacher: Proclaiming Womanist Rhetoric from the Pulpit.* Lanham, MD: Lexington Books, 2017.

Jones, Martha S. *Birthright Citizens: A History of Race and Rights in Antebellum America.* Cambridge: Cambridge University Press, 2018.

Jones, Rodney H. *Discourse Analysis: A Resources Book for Students.* 2nd ed. New York: Routledge, 2019.

Joseph, Celucien L. "Toward a Black African Theological Anthropology and Ubuntu Ethics." *Journal of Religion and Theology* 2, no. 1 (2018): 16–30.

Kantrowitz, Stephen. *More Than Freedom: Fighting for Black Citizenship in a White Republic, 1829–1889.* New York: Penguin Press, 2012.

Karenga, Maulana. "Nommo, Kawaida, and Communicative Practice." In *Understanding African American Rhetoric: Classical Origins to Contemporary Innovations*, edited by Ronald L. Jackson and Elain B. Johnson, 3–22. New York: Routledge, 2003.

Kaye, Anthony E. "Neighborhoods and Nat Turner: The Making of a Slave Rebel and the Unmaking of a Slave Rebellion." *Journal of the Early Republic* 27, no. 4 (Winter 2007): 705–20.

Kaylor, Brian. "Accounting for the Divine: Examining Rhetorical Claims of God's Inspiration." *Journal of Communication and Religion* 34 no. 1 (May 2011): 75–87.

Klumpp, James F., and Thomas A. Hollihan. "Rhetorical Criticism as Moral Action." *Quarterly Journal of Speech* 75, no. 1 (February 1989): 84–96.

Knowles-Borishade, Adetokunbo F. "Paradigm for Classical African Orature: Instrument for a Scientific Revolution?" *Journal of Black Studies* 21, no. 4 (June 1991): 488–500.

Lee, Jarena. "The Life and Religious Experience of Jarena Lee, a Coloured Lady: Giving Account of Her Call to Preach the Gospel." In *Sisters of the Spirit: Three Black Women's Autobiographies of the Nineteenth Century*, edited by William L. Andrews, 25–48. Bloomington: Indiana University Press, 1986.

Logan, Shirley Wilson. *"We Are Coming": The Persuasive Discourse of Nineteenth-Century Black Women.* Carbondale: Southern Illinois University Press, 1999.

Logue, Cal M. "Transcending Coercion: The Communicative Strategies of Black Slaves on Antebellum Plantations." *Quarterly Journal of Speech* 67, no. 1 (1981): 31–46.

Lomax, Tamura. *Jezebel Unhinged: Loosing the Black Female Body in Religion and Culture.* Durham, NC: Duke University Press, 2018.

Madlock, Annette D. "Introduction to the Special Issue." In "A Womanist Rhetorical Vision for Building the Beloved Community," edited by Annette D. Madlock. Special issue, *Journal of Communication and Religion* 43, no. 3 (Autumn 2020): 5–8.

Majocha, Kristen Lynn. "Prophetic Rhetoric: A Gap between the Field of Study and the Real World." *Journal of Communication and Religion* 39, no. 4 (Winter 2016): 5–18.

May, Nicholas. "Holy Rebellion: Religious Assembly Laws in Antebellum South Carolina and Virginia." *American Journal of Legal History* 49, no. 3 (July 2007): 237–56.

McClish, Glen. "William G. Allen's 'Orators and Oratory': Inventional Amalgamation, Pathos, and the Characterization of Violence in African-American Abolitionist Rhetoric." *Rhetoric Society Quarterly* 35, no. 1 (Winter 2005): 47–72.

McDonald, Nicole. "From Resistance to Receiving: A Rhetorical Analysis of the Call Narrative of Julia A. J. Foote." *Listening: Journal of Communication, Ethics, Religion, and Culture* 55, no. 3 (Fall 2020): 220–25.

McGee, Michael Calvin. "The 'Ideograph': A Link between Rhetoric and Ideology." In *Readings in Rhetorical Criticism*, 5th ed., edited by Carl R. Burgchardt and Hillary A. Jones, 466–79. State College: Strata, 2017.

McKerrow, Raymie E. "Critical Rhetoric: Theory and Praxis." In *Readings in Rhetorical Criticism*, 5th ed., edited by Carl R. Burgchardt and Hillary A. Jones, 81–101. State College: Strata, 2017.

Miller, Carolyn R. "Genre as Social Action." *Quarterly Journal of Speech* 70, no. 2 (1984): 56–72.

Moody, Jocelyn. *Sentimental Confession*. Athens: University of Georgia Press, 2001.

Muhammad, Khalil Gibran. *The Condemnation of Blackness: Race, Crime, and the Making of Modern Urban America*. Cambridge, MA: Harvard University Press, 2010.

Myers, William H. *God's Yes Was Louder Than My No: Rethinking the African American Call to Ministry*. Eugene, OR: Wipf and Stock, 1994.

Nash, Gary B. "New Light on Richard Allen: The Early Years of Freedom." *William and Mary Quarterly* 46, no. 2 (April 1989): 332–40.

Newman, Richard S. *Freedom's Prophet: Bishop Richard Allen, the AME Church, and the Black Founding Fathers*. New York: New York University Press, 2008.

Oates, Stephen B. *The Fires of Jubilee: Nat Turner's Fierce Rebellion*. New York: HarperCollins, 1990.

Ogbar, Jeffrey Ogbonna Green. "Prophet Nat and God's Children of Darkness: Black Religious Nationalism." *Journal of Religious Thought* 53–54, no. 2–1 (1991): 51–52.

O'Leary, Steven D. "A Dramatistic Theory of Apocalyptic Rhetoric." *Quarterly Journal of Speech* 79 (1999): 385–426.

Overall, Joel. "Piano and Pen: Music as Kenneth Burke's Secular Conversion." *Rhetoric Society Quarterly* 41, no. 5 (2011): 439–54.

Patterson, Robert J. "A Triple-Twined Re-appropriation: Womanist Theology and Gendered-Racial Protest in the Writings of Jarena Lee, Frances E. W. Harper, and Harriet Jacobs." *Religion and Literature* 45, no. 2 (Summer 2013): 55–82.

Pelletier, Kevin. *Apocalyptic Sentimentalism*. Athens: University of Georgia Press, 2015.

Pelletier, Kevin. "David Walker, Harriet Beecher Stowe, and the Logic of Sentimental Terror." *African American Review* 46, no. 2–3 (Summer–Fall 2013): 255–69.

Pohl, Christine D. *Making Room: Recovering Hospitality as a Christian Tradition*. Grand Rapids, MI: William B. Eerdmans, 1999.

Quintilian. *Quintilian on the Teaching of Speaking and Writing*. Edited by James J. Murphy. Carbondale: Southern Illinois University Press, 1987.

Raboteau, A. J. *Slave Religion: The Invisible Institution in the American South*. Oxford: Oxford University Press, 1978.

Richardson, Marilyn. *Maria Stewart: America's First Black Political Writer*. Bloomington: Indiana University Press, 1987.

Robinson, Elaine. *Race and Theology*. Nashville, TN: Abingdon Press, 2012.

Royster, Jacqueline Jones. "Introduction: Marking Trails in Studies of Race, Gender, and Culture." In *Calling Cards: Theory and Practice in the Study of Race, Gender, and Culture*, edited by Jacqueline Jones Royster and Ann Marie Mann Simpkins. Albany: State University of New York Press, 2005. Kindle.

Royster, Jacqueline Jones, and Gesa E. Kirsch. *Feminist Rhetorical Practices: New Horizons for Rhetoric, Composition, and Literacy Studies*. Carbondale: Southern Illinois University Press, 2012.

Ryan, Mary P. *Women in Public: Between Banner and Ballots, 1825–1880*. Baltimore, MD: John Hopkins University Press, 1990.

Santoro, Anthony. "The Prophet in His Own Words: Nat Turner's Biblical Construction." *Virginia Magazine of History and Biography* 116, no. 2 (2008): 114–49.

Sarna, Nahum. *Genesis: The JPS Torah Commentary*. Philadelphia, PA: Jewish Publication Society, 1989.

Schultze, Quentin J. "The 'God-Problem' in Communication Studies." *Journal of Communication and Religion* 28, no. 1 (March 2005): 1–22.

Schultze, Quentin J. "The Nature and Future of Religious Communication Scholarship." *Journal of Communication and Religion* 33, no. 2 (November 2010): 190–205.

Scully, Randolf Ferguson. "'I Come Here Before You and I Shall Not Go Away': Race, Gender, and Evangelical Community on the Eve of the Nat Turner Rebellion." *Journal of the Early Republic* 27, no. 4 (Winter 2007): 721–28.

Shalom-Guy, Hava. "The Call Narratives of Gideon and Moses: Literary Convention or More?" *Journal of Hebrew Scriptures* 11 (2011): 1–19, https://doi.org/10.5508/jhs.2011.v11.a11.

Shiffrin, Steven H. "The Rhetoric of Black Violence in the Antebellum Period: Henry Highland Garnet." *Journal of Black Studies* 2, no. 1 (September 1971): 45–56.

Sidbury, James. "Reading, Revelation, and Rebellion: The Textual Communities of Gabriel, Denmark Vesey, and Nat Turner." In *Nat Turner: A Slave Rebellion in History and Memory*, edited by Kenneth S. Greenberg, 119–33. Oxford: Oxford University Press, 2002.

Stewart, Maria W. *The Productions of Mrs. Maria W. Stewart Presented to the First Africa Baptist Church and Society, of the City of Boston*. Boston, MA: Friends of Freedom and Virtue, 1835.

Stewart, Maria W. "What If I Am a Woman?" In *Lift Every Voice: African American Oratory, 1787–1900*, edited by Philip S. Foner and Robert James Branham, 135–42. Tuscaloosa: University of Alabama Press, 1998.

Stewart, Maria W. "Why Sit Ye Here and Die?" In *Lift Every Voice: African American Oratory, 1787–1900*, edited by Philip S. Foner and Robert James Branham, 125–29. Tuscaloosa: University of Alabama Press, 1998.

Sundquist, Eric J. *To Wake the Nations: Race in the Making of American Literature*. Cambridge, MA: Harvard University Press, 1993.

Taylor, Nikki M. *Driven toward Madness: The Fugitive Slave Margaret Garner and Tragedy on the Ohio*. Athens: Ohio University Press, 2016.

Taylor, Steven. "The Political Influence of African American Ministers: A Legacy of West African Culture." *Journal of Black Studies* 37, no. 1 (September 2006): 5–19.

Townes, Emilie M. *Womanist Justice, Womanist Hope*. American Academy of Religion Academy Series 79. Atlanta, GA: Scholars Press, 1993.

Turner, Nat. *"The Confessions of Nat Turner" and Related Documents*. Edited by Kenneth S. Greenberg. Boston, MA: St. Martin's Press, 1996.

von Rad, Gerhard. *The Message of the Prophets*. New York: Harper and Row, 1965.

Walker, Alice. *In Search of Our Mother's Gardens*. San Diego: Harcourt Brace Jovanovich, 1983.

Walton, John H. *The Lost World of Genesis One*. Downers Grove: InterVarsity Press, 2009.

Waters, Kristin. *Maria W. Stewart and the Roots of Black Political Thought*. Jackson: University Press of Mississippi, 2022.

Watkins-Dickerson, Dianna N. "'You Are Somebody': A Study of the Prophetic Rhetoric of Rev. Henry Logan Starks, DMin." *Journal of Communication and Religion* 43, no. 4 (Winter 2020): 92–107.

Wesley, John. *The Works of John Wesley*. 3rd ed. Vol. 5. London: Wesleyan Methodist Book Room, 1872.

Westermann, Claus. *Basic Forms of Prophetic Speech*. Translated by Hugh Clayton White. Louisville, KY: Westminster / John Knox Press, 1991.

Wichelns, Herbert A. "The Literary Criticism of Oratory." In *The Rhetorical Idiom: Essays in Rhetoric, Oratory, Language, and Drama*, edited by Donald C. Bryant, 5–42. Ithaca: Cornell University Press, 1958.

Wichelns, Herbert A. "The Literary Criticism of Oratory." In *Readings in Rhetorical Criticism*, 5th ed., edited by Carl R. Burgchardt and Hillary A. Jones, 3–27. State College: Strata, 2017.

Wiesel, Elie. *Night*. Rev. ed. Translated by Marion Wiesel. New York: Hill and Wang, 2006.

Williams, Reggie L. *Bonhoeffer's Black Jesus: Harlem Renaissance Theology and an Ethic of Resistance*. Waco: Baylor University Press, 2014.

Wimbush, Vincent L. "Introduction: Interpretating Resistance, Resisting Interpretations." *Semeia* 79 (1997): 1–10.

Woodyard, Kerith M. "Depatriarchalizing in Rhetorical Theory: Toward a Feminist Prophetic Tradition." *Ohio Communication Journal* 48 (October 2010): 27–42.

Woodyard, Kerith M. "'If by Martyrdom I Can Advance My Race One Step, I Am Ready for It': Prophetic Ethos and the Reception of Elizabeth Cady Stanton's *The Woman's Bible*." *Journal of Communication and Religion* 31, no. 2 (November 2008): 272–326.

Woolridge, Nancy Bullock. "The Slave Preacher—Portrait of a Leader." *Journal of Negro Education* 14, no. 1 (Winter 1945): 28–37.

Wright, Jeremiah. "(2003) Rev. Jeremiah Wright, 'Confusing God and Government.'" BlackPast, May 6, 2008. https://www.blackpast.org/african-american-history/2008-rev-jeremiah-wright-confusing-god-and-government/.

Index

About the Author

Thomas M. Fuerst holds a PhD in rhetoric from the University of Memphis. His interests lie in the intersection of religious studies, theology, biblical studies, and rhetoric. His dissertation won the 2022 Religious Communication Association's Dissertation of the Year Award. He currently lives in Memphis, Tennessee, with his wife and four children, where he pastors Memphis First United Methodist Church.

Printed in the United States
by Baker & Taylor Publisher Services